D0204688

John Milton
The Prose Works

Twayne's English Authors Series

Arthur Kinney, Editor

TEAS 546

JOHN MILTON
By courtesy of the National Portrait Gallery, London

John Milton
The Prose Works

Thomas N. Corns

University of Wales, Bangor

Twayne Publishers

New York

Twayne's English Authors Series No. 546

John Milton: The Prose Works
Thomas N. Corns

Twayne Publishers

1633 Broadway
New York, NY 10019

Library of Congress Cataloging-in-Publication Data

Corns, Thomas N.
    John Milton : the prose works / Thomas N. Corns.
        p.   cm. — (Twayne's English authors series ; TEAS 546)
    Includes bibliographical references and index.
    ISBN 0-8057-4530-0 (alk. paper)
    1. Milton, John, 1608–1674—Prose. 2. English prose literature—
Early modern, 1500–1700—History and criticism. 3. Didactic
literature, English—History and criticism. 4. Great Britain—
Civilization—17th century—Sources. I. Title. II. Series.
PR3592.P7C67   1998
828'.408—dc21   97-36419
                                                                          CIP

This paper meets the requirements of ANSI/NISO Z3948–1992 (Permanence of Paper).

10 9 8 7 6 5 4 3 2

Printed in the United States of America

To Pat, for patience

Contents

Editor's Note

Thomas N. Corns's illuminating study of the prose works of John Milton places all of that major writer's English and Latin prose works—from his earliest student exercises to his posthumous works including the controversial *De Doctrina Christiana*—in the strife-torn period that inspired them. In examining Milton's writing against the religious battles, the regicide, and the civil war that marked the mid-seventeenth century in England, Corns shows how Milton's courage in defending the execution of Charles I and the republic of Oliver Cromwell gave to the age some of its most enduring works of debate and endangered Milton's very life. He was outspoken in the divorce tracts that pushed him outside the pale of Puritan respectability. He never wavered in his eloquent defense of regicide and republican government. He was among the last to defend in print the Good Old Cause. Even in the Restoration, Corns writes, "he endured prosecution and suspicion until circumstances permitted one last blast of his trumpet; even in death his literary legacy was hunted out and suppressed." In this study, one of the most respected authorities on Milton's prose contextualizes it in ways that not only help us to understand the life of the poet who lost his sight while writing for what he believed in, but put into a new perspective many of Milton's poetic works, including *Comus, Lycidas, Paradise Lost, Paradise Regained,* and *Samson Agonistes*. This comprehensive examination will serve both newcomer and seasoned scholar in the detail of its argument and the richness of its insight.

Arthur F. Kinney

Acknowledgments

I am happy to acknowledge the kind permission of Yale University Press to reproduce material from the *Complete Prose Works of John Milton,* edited by Don M. Wolfe et al. (New Haven: Yale University Press, 1953-1982); and of Addison Wesley Longman to reproduce material from *The Poems of John Milton,* edited by John Carey and Alastair Fowler (London: Longman, 1968). Except where stated, all references to Milton's works are to these two editions, hereafter cited as *CPW* and *Poems.* In the case of volume VII of *CPW,* all references are to the revised edition.

I should also like to thank Arthur Kinney for his encouragement and editorial contribution and Linda Jones for helping in numerous ways in the final preparation of the typescript. Finally, I am grateful to Gordon Campbell for reading a late draft and making many helpful comments.

Chronology

1608   Milton born on 9 December, first surviving child of John Milton Senior, a scrivener living in the city of London, and Ann Milton.

1618   The Thirty Years' War begins, initially involving the Catholic Holy Roman Empire in conflict with Bohemia, its Protestant possession, and soon drawing in the German Protestant state of the Palatinate, whose ruler, Frederick, is the son-in-law of James I. The conflict widens to include Denmark, Sweden, and most of the states of what is modern Germany and by 1635 brings Catholic France into the war on the side of the Protestant states. What is contemporaneously recognized in England as a war of religion combines with the greatest struggle hitherto for the European balance of power. England stays out of the war.

1620   The Battle of the White Mountain, in which Imperial forces rout Frederick and crush the Bohemian rebellion.

The Pilgrim Fathers establish a colony in New England.

Milton probably enters St. Paul's School, London.

1625   The death of James I and the accession of Charles I to the kingdoms of England, Scotland, and Ireland. Milton enters Christ's College, Cambridge.

1628   William Laud is advanced to the see of London.

1629   Charles I dismisses the last English Parliament to meet before 1640.

Milton is admitted to the degree of Bachelor of Arts. He writes, but does not publish, "On the Morning of Christ's Nativity."

1632   Milton is admitted to the degree of Master of Arts. His first publication, the poem "On Shakespeare," appears as part of the prefatory material to the Second Folio of Shakespeare's works. He leaves Cambridge to return to the household of his father at Hammersmith and Horton, where he lives without gainful employment until 1638.

1633   Laud becomes Archbishop of Canterbury.

1634   Milton's masque, *Comus,* is performed at Ludlow as part of the celebrations of the installation of the Earl of Bridgewater as President of the Council of Wales.

William Prynne, a leading Puritan activist, is tried, mutilated, and imprisoned for attacking masques.

1637   The judicial mutilation and subsequent incarceration of Puritan activists Prynne (already in prison), Henry Burton, and John Bastwick.

Milton's *Comus* is published for the first time.

Milton's Cambridge contemporary Edward King is drowned in a shipwreck. Milton composes an elegy for him, "Lycidas," first published in a commemorative volume in 1638.

1638   Milton leaves England for an extended visit to France and Italy, returning in 1639.

John Lilburne, a Puritan activist, is flogged through London and subsequently incarcerated.

1639   Charles I attempts to discipline his kingdom of Scotland, thus beginning a political and economic crisis that finally compels him to call an English Parliament.

Milton sets up house in London.

1640   The English Parliament meets briefly (the Short Parliament), and then a second Parliament (the Long Parliament) is called after further crises in Charles I's relations with Scotland.

The Long Parliament impeaches Thomas Wentworth, Earl of Strafford, Charles's chief minister through the previous decade, together with William Laud, the Archbishop of Canterbury. The former is tried and executed in 1641, the latter in 1645.

1641   In the kingdom of Ireland, an insurrection by the Catholic majority against Protestant settlers and the Protestant ascendancy results in considerable suffering and loss of life among the Protestants.

Milton publishes *Of Reformation, Of Prelatical Episcopacy,* and *Animadversions.*

1642 Milton publishes *The Reason of Church Government* and *Apology.*

The First Civil War begins. The Battle of Edgehill, the first major engagement, produces a stalemate. The royalists march on London, pulling back when confronted by Parliamentary militia at Turnham Green.

Milton marries Mary Powell, his first wife, who returns shortly afterwards to her father's household.

London theaters are closed.

1643 The Westminster Assembly of Divines convenes.

Milton publishes *The Doctrine and Discipline of Divorce.*

1644 The Parliamentary victory at the Battle of Marston Moor gives Parliament an advantage in the war.

Milton publishes *Of Education, Areopagitica,* and *Bucer* and reissues *Doctrine and Discipline* in a second, extended, edition.

1645 The Parliamentary armies are re-formed into the New Model Army under the command of Thomas Fairfax, with Oliver Cromwell as his deputy. The First Civil War is effectively concluded by the Parliamentary victory at the Battle of Naseby.

Milton publishes *Tetrachordon, Colasterion,* and *The Poems of Mr. John Milton.* His wife returns to his household.

1646 The New Model Army mops up remaining areas of royalist resistance. Charles I surrenders to the Scots.

The birth of Ann, Milton's first child.

1647 The Scots hand Charles I over to the English Parliament. Relations between Parliament and the New Model Army deteriorate, and the army occupies London.

1648 The Second Civil War begins as hostilities break out in several parts of England and in Wales. Charles I taken into the custody of the New Model Army. The Long Parliament is purged of members hostile to the leaders of the New Model Army, as Cromwell emerges clearly as the most powerful figure in English politics and as his commander in chief, Fairfax, becomes increasingly marginalized.

The birth of Mary, Milton's second child.

The Treaty of Westphalia concludes the Thirty Years' War.

1649   The trial and execution of Charles I. The new republic faces a grave crisis as the warring factions in Ireland settle their differences and acknowledge Charles II as King and as Scotland, which had supported the English Parliament militarily in the First Civil War, also acknowledges Charles II and prepares to invade England.

Dissension between senior officers and junior ranks sympathetic to the Leveler cause of radical reform becomes acute, resulting in the Burford Mutiny, which Cromwell suppresses. Gerrard Winstanley and the Diggers establish a short-lived agrarian commune on St. George's Hill, near Cobham, Surrey.

Cromwell's expeditionary force to Ireland meets with a series of victories. The towns of Drogheda and Wexford are stormed and thousands of inhabitants are massacred.

Milton is appointed Secretary of Foreign Tongues to the Council of State.

Milton publishes *The Tenure of Kings and Magistrates, Observations,* and *Eikonoklastes.*

1650   Cromwell's expeditionary force to Scotland beats the Scots at the Battle of Dunbar.

Milton's sight deteriorates rapidly.

1651   Cromwell's force crushes the Scots at the Battle of Worcester, and Charles II flees into exile.

Milton publishes the *First Defense of the English People.*

His third child, John, is born.

1652   Inception of the First Anglo-Dutch War.

Milton's fourth child, Deborah, is born. His son, John, and his first wife die.

Milton is now totally blind.

1653   The purged Long Parliament is dismissed, and Cromwell becomes Lord Protector.

1654   The First Anglo-Dutch War ends on terms favorable to England.

Milton publishes the *Second Defense*.

1655   Milton publishes his *Defense of Himself*.

1656   Milton marries Katherine Woodcock.

1657   Milton's fifth child, Katherine, is born.

1658   Oliver Cromwell dies; his son Richard is appointed Lord Protector in his place.

Milton's second wife and Katherine, his youngest child, die.

1659   Milton publishes *Civil Power* and *Hirelings*.

The end of the Protectorate.

1660   Milton drafts several arguments against the restoration of the monarchy and publishes *The Readie and Easie Way* (two editions) and *Brief Notes*. Charles II is restored, and Milton is imprisoned for a time.

1661   Louis XIV assumes full control of France.

1663   Milton marries his third and last wife, Elizabeth Minshull; she will survive him.

1665   The Second Anglo-Dutch War begins; the outbreak of the Great Plague drives Milton from London.

1666   The Great Fire of London.

1667   Charles II is forced to conclude the Second Anglo-Dutch War on unfavorable terms.

Milton publishes the first edition of *Paradise Lost*.

1669   Milton publishes *Accedence Commenc't Grammar*.

1670   Milton publishes *History of Britain*.

1671   Milton publishes *Paradise Regained* and *Samson Agonistes* as a double volume.

1672   Milton publishes the *Art of Logic*.

1673   Milton publishes *Of True Religion* and *Poems, &c, upon Several Occasions*, the second edition of his minor poems.

1674   Milton publishes his *Familiar Letters and Academic Exercises* and the second edition of *Paradise Lost*.

        Milton dies on or about 8 November.

Chapter One
A Biographical Introduction

In most respects, the life records relating to John Milton, the documentary evidence that survives him, are wholly typical of his age and class.[1] We know when and probably where he was born. We know the names and social status of his parents and grandparents. His college records are extant. For some periods the evidence is thin—especially, perhaps, for the decade or so after he left the university. Sometimes, as in the case of his European travels, almost all we have is his own probably tendentious accounts. After his return to England, the records gradually become more frequent. We know when he married and remarried, when his children were born and died, and when his wives died. Once he enters the civil service of the English republic, he leaves a trace in the records of that succession of governments. We have some memoirs of him by his contemporaries, particularly in the period of his public employment, and after his death brief lives were written, some of them evidently by people close to him. What we do not have is an account that discloses any of the interiority of his personality. His extant letters are overwhelmingly formal. He left no journal. He wrote no spiritual autobiography; indeed, the autobiographical episodes in his prose writing usually serve some immediate exigency of his polemic. The memoirs of him tell us little about his deeper passions and motivations. Moreover, in ways that should be discouraging to the more speculative biographer, the kinds of writing he was drawn to—in poetry, preeminently, biblical narratives; in prose, the controversial genres—generally preclude the personal, confessional modes.

In the absence of hard evidence, more speculative biographers have postulated vivid hypotheses of some psychological complexity.[2] Indeed, even the most skeptical account may discern in the literary legacy and the life records something of the man himself. His self-confidence and self-regard are inscribed in his bold appropriation into English of the most esteemed classical genre, epic; in the way in which, in his poetry, he sought comparison with Homer and Virgil; in his zeal in his prose to engage the most distinguished opponents his enemies could field. His pugnacity is evident in his prose, and his courage appears clearly if we examine the sometimes perilous circumstances under which he wrote. But let us focus, briefly, on the facts.

He was born on 9 December 1608, the eldest surviving child of John Milton Senior, a scrivener living in the City of London. Scriveners were originally copyists or penmen who prepared copies especially of legal documents, but by the early seventeenth century they approximated financial advisers, often engaged in arranging loans or placing investments for their clients. John Milton Senior was not a poor man, and in the extant records we have no sense that Milton ever experienced material deprivation.

His father, though not educated to degree level, had some cultural refinement; he was an accomplished minor composer, some of whose work is extant. His political and religious orientation is sometimes the subject of speculation, but we really know very little about it. Milton's younger brother, Christopher, a lawyer, was a royalist supporter who achieved professional advancement under the restored Stuarts after 1660. We may not confidently assert that Milton was straightforwardly the Puritan product of a Puritan home. Of Milton's own early political and religious preferences, we have only the doubtful evidence of his early poetry, which some critics regard as indicative of Puritan leanings and others as wholly in accord with the more conservative elements then dominant within the Church of England.

Milton apparently lived in the family home until he went to Cambridge at the age of 17 (not particularly young by contemporary standards). He was fortunate in that he lived very close to St. Paul's School, which offered as good an education as was then available institutionally, and we know his schooling was supplemented by private tuition from Thomas Young, an energetic Scottish divine currently living in London who later became a prominent moderate Puritan activist. In 1625 Milton entered Christ's College, Cambridge, where he seems to have prospered academically. On leaving with the degree of Master of Arts, he returned to the family home, which had now removed from the City of London to its environs. He stayed there, writing some poetry and reading a great deal, until he left, possibly somewhat hurriedly, for an extended Continental tour (1638–1639), which took him to Italy. He left as a minor poet of some distinction—some of his poems had appeared in collections, and his masque, *Comus,* had been published in 1637. His poem on the death of Edward King, "Lycidas," shows at least a nascent opposition to the ceremonialism of the Caroline Church of England. He retired once more until 1641, when he published his first political pamphlet, *Of Reformation*, a scathing assault on the role of bishops in England. The decade of the 1640s witnessed Milton's gradual radicalization. First he attacked the bishops. Then, as the control of the church passed from their hands, he advocated a sweeping reform of the law relating to divorce. (He himself had married, unsuccessfully, for the first time in 1642.) The moderate Puritans who had replaced the episcopalians as the masters of state religion took a poor view of so bold a proposal, and Milton became associated with more radical activists, the Independents, an association that was to continue until 1660. In the mid-1640s, as Parliament's armies were securing victory over the forces of Charles I, Milton wrote a series of pamphlets advocating greater toleration of heterodox ideas and restating his divorce proposals. In this period, he also published his first collection of poems.

In the late 1640s the Independents, thanks largely to support from Oliver Cromwell and the army officers in his circle, displaced more moderate Puritans from power, purging from parliament those who opposed them. Charles I, who had been beaten on the battlefield, was brought to trial and executed in January 1649. Milton, who had some notoriety in the mid-1640s, emerged as one of the two most eloquent defenders of the new republic. (The other was the journalist Marchamont Needham.) In 1649 and the 1650s he wrote pamphlets in English and Latin defending the execution of the King. For the first time in his life he took regular employment, accepting the post of Latin secretary to successive republican governments. He worked in effect in the foreign office, translating and drafting diplomatic documents and participating in the government of England as an active and high-ranking civil servant, for which he was well paid.

However, his personal life was not without tragedy. From the late 1640s his eyesight had started to deteriorate, and by 1652 he was completely blind. The diagnosis is not certain, but glaucoma seems the likeliest explanation. In 1652 his first wife died, shortly after the death of his only son; three daughters survived from the marriage. He married again, but his second wife and the child of that marriage died in 1658. (His third wife, whom he married in 1663, survived him by more than 50 years; the marriage was childless.) The political causes to which he had devoted himself began to disintegrate in the late 1650s, and in 1660 he wrote a short and desperate series of pamphlets urging the retention of republican government. At the restoration of Charles II to his father's throne in 1660, Milton's prospects were unpromising. He lost much of his personal fortune, which he had held in government bonds that the new regime would not honor. However, he was spared prolonged incarceration or execution to the surprise of some of his contemporaries, who thought that so prominent a republican activist merited severe punishment.

The rest of his life was spent in retirement, although he ventured to publish some politically motivated prose in the early 1670s. He published his most significant poetry during the period after the Restoration, *Paradise Lost* in 1667 (reissued in a second edition in 1674) and *Paradise Regained* with *Samson Agonistes* in 1671. He was never rehabilitated politically and was apparently always anxious about assassination by royalists disappointed about his survival. He died in London in 1674, about a month before his 66th birthday.

Chapter Two
Academic Exercises

John Milton's Latin exercises, preserved from his student days, appeared first in the last prose volume published in his lifetime, a collection bearing the title page *Joannis Miltonii Angli, Epistolarum Familiarium Liber Unus: Quibus Accesserunt, Eiusdem, iam olim in Collegio Adolescentis, Prolusiones Quaedam Oratoriae* (that is, *One book of letters to friends by John Milton, Englishman; to which are added certain prolusions of the same writer done in college when he was still a youth*). To the letters we shall return shortly. My immediate concern is with what are usually termed the *Prolusions* or *Academic Exercises*.

At the time of their publication, 1674, Milton was in his 66th and final year. He had preserved the texts for more than 40 years, which shows a remarkable concern with the survival of the products—all the products—of his own pen. This action characterizes his attitude toward his own writing throughout his career. In the 1640s, as he writes vernacular prose works, he takes care to ensure their survival in England's major university library, the Bodleian at Oxford, sending copies to replace those burned by royalists.[1] He also makes sure to present copies to George Thomason, who was contemporaneously building a huge collection of publications, which documents well the developing crises of the mid-century.[2] We can see Milton's almost obsessive concern in his response to those adversaries who misquote his prose even slightly.[3] So we should not be surprised to learn that he had preserved university work of his adolescence into his old age.

Lest he seem hopelessly and foolishly vain, three qualifications are needed. First, Milton was by no means the only seventeenth-century author to publish his student essays in his maturity. The royalist poet John Cleveland included his own academic orations and exercises in his collected works.[4] This was an age in which accomplishment in Latin was valued, almost irrespective of the content of the text. Second, the closing years of Milton's life, like the period after it, saw considerable interest among publishers in bringing out even small pieces of Milton's writing, given their sense of the reading public's interest in the internationally notorious figure that Milton had, through his republican writings, become. Finally, the initiative to publish the Latin university pieces clearly came from his publisher, Brabazon Aylmer, rather than the author. Aylmer had intended that his little double volume should offer the Restoration reading public a collection both of Milton's private letters to his intimates and some of the Latin letters he had drafted in the 1650s on behalf of the English Republic, which he served as a civil servant associated with foreign policy. The mid-1670s saw a concerted attempt by the restored monarchy and its servants to curtail publication of Milton's writings, and as Aylmer's preface to the 1674 edition makes clear, he had been effectively frightened off:

> I had some time since conceived the hope, gentle reader, that the letters of this Author, both public and private, might be entrusted to me to be printed in a single volume. But when I learnt that those who had the sole rights objected, for certain reasons, to the issue of the public letters, I decided to rest content with such part as was permitted and to publish the private letters alone.[5]

A collection of Milton's state papers eventually saw publication in Amsterdam shortly after his death, despite the attempts of English government agents to prevent posthumous publication of potentially sensitive material.[6] These events indicate something of Milton's contemporary status as failed revolutionary and remnant of the great experiment of the English revolution, a status earned not for his achievements as the poet of *Paradise Lost* but for his prose writings, preeminently those justifying the killing of Charles I, to which we turn in chapters 5 and 6. He had become a man fascinating not only to an English readership but to a continental European readership as well.

Aylmer found his project undermined by the government veto on the use of state papers associated with Milton, but as a resourceful entrepreneur he sought to save the situation and to produce in his own word a "saleable" volume:

> Finding . . . that [the letters to friends] were somewhat too few to form a volume of reasonable size, I decided to treat with the author through a common friend and obtain his sanction to the publication in addition of any small work he might chance to have kept by him, to fill up the space and compensate for the paucity of the letters. This friend prevailed upon him to look through his papers, scattered among which he eventually chanced upon these youthful productions, and yielded to his friend's importunity regarding them.[7]

It is improbable that many today read those early exercises with much delight in their wit or stylistic felicity, either in Latin or in translation, and we may recognize the limits of their appeal for earlier generations by the fact that, although they have been reprinted several times, subsequent editions before that of 1932 have simply reprinted the misprints that pepper the original text,[8] lending some strength to David Masson's conclusion that "they do not seem ever to have been read" before his account of them.[9]

I entertain no expectation of reviving a genuine affection for this part of the prose oeuvre. However, a consideration of them helps a modern reader identify potent elements in Milton's mature prose, both in Latin and English; the child Milton is emphatically the father of the man.

We do not know exactly how the seven exercises printed in Aylmer's volume fitted into the career of John Milton at the University of Cambridge between 1625 and 1632, although we know which were delivered in his college and which in the "public schools" of the university; only one, the Fourth of 1628, can be dated with certainty, although intelligent reconstructions have been attempted from time to time. Masson may well have got it about right when he concluded:

> Of these seven exercises, three, it will be seen, were read or recited in the public schools . . . forming, doubtless, a portion of the statutory exercises required there. Three others . . . were read or recited in College, also according to regulation; the title of the last seeming to indicate that it was the "declamation" required as the last exercise in College before the M.A. degree. The sixth exercise stands by itself, as a voluntary discourse delivered by appointment at a meeting of the students of Christ's and of other youths of the University, held, by way of frolic, in the autumn holidays.[10]

Then, as now, Cambridge was a collegiate university, and Milton, like others, would have been obliged to perform certain tasks for assessment both within his college and at the university level. In the early modern period (as for some while before), these tasks took the form of oral examinations, in which candidates were required to defend, in Latin, theses or arguments assigned to them. Such defenses took the form of formal expositions and of responses to arguments raised against them. The emphasis of the assessment would seem to have been not on the quality of the content but on the eloquence of its exposition and on the skill with which arguments were organized and presented and contrary positions engaged and refuted.

Here in Milton's adolescence and young manhood, we see his thorough grounding in some of the essentials of controversial prose of the kind he would later write as part of real and urgent debate. Note, for example, that Milton's performance reflects a training in arguing even diametrically opposed positions. The First Prolusion engages the "debate" (if the term does not flatter it) "Whether Day or Night is the More Excellent" (*CPW,* I, 218). He concludes, as no doubt was his instruction, in favor of Day; doubtless an adversary spoke for Night, as Milton could as easily have done himself. The briefs assigned are arbitrary, the arguments unimportant, and the outcome of no significance.

Indeed, several times we find Milton engaged in expositions that reflect the assumptions and methods of the scholastic philosophy of the late middle ages that was still so influential in English academic life in the early modern period, despite the incipient rise of the new science associated with Francis Bacon. That scholastic philosophy finds expression in the endless elaboration and perfection of the received wisdom of the ancient world, preeminently Aristotle. Thus we find Milton elaborating (as no doubt was required of him) several thoroughly scholastic positions, speaking "On the Harmony of the Spheres" (Prolusion Two, *CPW,* I, 234–39), arguing that "In the Destruction of any Substance there can be no Resolution into First Matter" (Prolusion Four, *CPW,* I, 249–56), and defending that proposition that "There are no partial Forms in an Animal in addition to the Whole" (Prolusion Five, *CPW,* I, 257–64). Even the most learned of twentieth-century Miltonists find elements of these disquisitions baffling, so embedded are they in the thinking, knowledge, and assumptions of an earlier age. But Milton himself not only wrote them but preserved them and vouchsafed them to a reading public. In the long tradition of Milton criticism there recurs a liberal impulse to resolve contradictions, both apparent and real, within his writing by identifying whatever looks progressive to liberal notions of progress as "what Milton really meant" and by relegating whatever is regressive or conservative or politically unacceptable to a modern readership as in some ways uttered with less conviction, assumed for the immediate exigencies of debate, or spoken in a self-contradictory fashion that indicates to the *cognoscenti* their author's unmistakable place among the angels of liberal enlightenment. Thus, when Milton in Prolusion Three produces "An Attack on the Scholastic Philosophy" (*CPW,* I, 240–48), the temptation is to value this as his authentic opinion, as "the way in which Milton reacted to the educational system at Cambridge."[11]

But we should beware of the impulse to produce a single Miltonic voice and the wish to find the heroic Milton in all his utterances. We have inherited a complex oeuvre, deeply embedded in Milton's own age and profoundly shaped by literary and polemical contexts. On issues rather more profound than the advantages of Day over Night (or Night over Day), Milton adopts contradictory views at different times and occasionally at about the same time. On kingship, for example, we find Milton, in *Of Reformation* (1641), seeking to defend it from the disgraces occasioned it by bishops; in 1649, in *The Tenure of Kings and Magistrates* and *Eikonoklastes,* he defends the trial and execution of Charles I; in his *Second Defense of the English People* (1654), he sings the praises of Queen Christina of Sweden like the most sycophantic royalist panegyrist. In the *Prolusions* of his student days, we find the first examples of the plurality of Miltonic ideology. How he perceives and represents the world is inextricably intertwined with the moment and the medium; that is the most important lesson of the *Prolusions* for his modern readers.

We may see, too, how well he had learned the rhetorician's lesson on the importance of securing and retaining the approval of one's readers, what the textbooks called the *captatio benevolentiae,* or the securing of good will. As Milton himself puts it at the start of Prolusion One, "It is a frequent maxim of the most eminent masters of rhetoric . . . that . . . the speaker must begin by winning the good-will of his audience" (*CPW,* I, 218). This imperative remains a feature of his mature prose both in Latin and in English. Thus, for example, *Areopagitica* opens with an address to the Long Parliament designed to convince its members of the "speaker's" respect and loyalty to them. Thus, too, *Eikonoklastes* begins by establishing a positive image of the speaker as a modest citizen reluctantly drawn to answering the late king. In the Prolusions, Milton's self-representation as an aspect of securing attention and good will plainly belongs to a more concrete frame of reference; he knows precisely whom he addresses because he sees them before him, and he brings to the work a sense of how they already perceive him:

> For how can I hope for your good-will, when . . . I encounter none but hostile glances, so that my task seems to be to placate the implacable?
> . . .
>   Yet . . . I see here and there, if I do not mistake, some who without a word show clearly by their looks how well they wish me. The approval of these is . . . precious to me. . . . (*CPW,* I, 219–20)

Here, in the implied context of apparent unpopularity, Milton attempts a preemptive maneuver and a division of the audience that permit him to identify an early manifestation of the fit audience, though few. Different situations require different strokes, and Milton can be almost obsequious to his hearers, as in Prolusion Two:

> If there is any room for an insignificant person like myself, Members of the University, after you have heard so many eminent speakers, I too will attempt, to the best of my small powers, to show my appreciation of this day's appointed celebrations, and to follow, though at a distance, the festal train of eloquence to-day. (*CPW,* I, 234)

In reading Milton's prose (and his poetry), we should never in facile fashion take the multiplicities of apparent revelations and appeals, the endless attempt to name, address and speak to his readers, at their face value. This is a writer well trained and deeply skilled in working his audience, much as a dog is trained to work sheep.

What is less clear from the exercises in the Aylmer volume is that such pieces were generally delivered in a controversial context. We have, if you like, the propositions; what we do not have are the responses and the response to the responses. We do, however, find Milton anticipating and meeting counterarguments to his propositions: "But my opponents have not even yet lost all hope of victory; for they are making a second attack, inferring from this that. . . . We, on the other hand, absolutely refuse to accept this inference, and in order to maintain our position unimpaired in spite of it, we draw this distinction, that . . ." (*CPW,* I, 255). Again, the mature prose lives off such close engagement of contrary positions; sometimes whole tracts, such as *Animadversions* or *Eikonoklastes,* amount to little more than a point-by-point rebuttal of an adversary, in which sections from the opponents' texts are followed by Milton's pointed rejoinder.

Readers of the *Prolusions* may be occasionally surprised by the vehemence with which controversy is engaged and with the grossness of the bantering humor that sometimes characterizes them:

> For my part, if I see anyone not opening his mouth as wide as he should to laugh, I shall say that he is trying to hide teeth which are foul and decayed, and yellow from neglect, or misplaced or projecting, or else that at to-day's feast he has so crammed his belly that he dares not put any extra strain upon it by laughing, for fear that not the Sphinx but his sphincter anus should sing a second part to his mouth's first and acciden-

> tally let out some enigmas, which I leave to the doctors instead of to Oedipus to explain. For I should not like the cheerful sound of laughter to be drowned by groans from the posterior in this assembly. (Prolusion Six, *CPW,* I, 278)

So anyone who doesn't laugh at Milton's jokes must be afraid to disclose dental problems or else can't laugh and control the anal sphincter at the same time, and the smells made would be pretty enigmatic; not the sort of enigma that is resolved by Oedipus answering the riddle of the Sphinx but the sort of enigma that is answered by the medical profession. Milton, future author of *Paradise Lost* and soon-to-be author of the Nativity Ode, turns a joke around farting. But this is not mere youthful behavior. Abrasive, vehement, and sometimes rather smutty elements surface persistently in his mature prose. Thus, Milton urges bishops, "Wipe your fat corpulencies out of our light" (*Animadversions, CPW,* I, 732), and tells his learned episcopalian adversary that his text is marked by "a more perfect and distinguishable odour of your socks" (*Animadversions, CPW,* I, 733). He remarks of the servant-turned-soliciter who opposed his divorce tracts, "I mean not to dispute Philosophy with this Pork, who never read any" (*Colasterion,* II, 737). Most notoriously, the Latin defenses of the Engish republic frequently mutate into extended assaults in this vein on those whom he believes himself to be refuting.

Milton's willingness to take up arguments that serve his immediate purpose, his occasionally ingratiating manner to his target readership, his commitment to sometimes rather nit-picking controversy, his persistently adversarial posture, and his surprising grossness—so much of what is hardest for a modern reader to appreciate in Milton's prose—are present in his earliest writing as part of the culture he inherited and the intellectual milieu in which he grew up. These aspects are as much a part of Milton's prose as are the noble sentiments and maxims inscribed on our public buildings.[12] We are separated from the early modern period by long ages of great reserve and politeness and we have expectations of a certain restraint in public life; but to see Milton's prose as it really is, not as polite opinion, we must return it to that more straightforwardly brutal period when eloquence, wit, and ingenuity joined with a savage aggression and an unscrupulous guile in the service of political commitment. Welcome to the seventeenth century.

Chapter Three
The Antiprelatical Pamphlets

We do not really know how or when or why Milton became a radical. In 1641, 10 years or so after he had made the decision not to enter holy orders, he described himself as someone who felt "Church-outed," exiled from a church whose authoritarianism and whose practices he could not accept (*The Reason of Church-Government, CPW,* I, 823). But the 1630s constitute a rather enigmatic decade in Milton's life records. Even though he left Cambridge in 1632, on his own account unable to serve the Church of England for ideological reasons, by 1634 he was collaborating with Henry Lawes, one of Charles I's favorite court musicians and composers, in the creation of *A Masque Performed at Ludlow Castle,* a courtly celebration of the installation of the Earl of Bridgewater in his high governmental role as President of Wales and the Marches. Evidently Milton's sense of alienation from the English establishment was scarcely uniform, and the masque itself must be squeezed very hard if it is to be read as in some way advancing an oppositional argument.[1]

In 1629 Charles I had abandoned Parliaments as part of his strategy for ruling his three kingdoms of England (including Wales), Scotland, and Ireland, not least because he had no enthusiasm for the kinds of criticism that would inevitably have been leveled against him in an English Parliament had one been convened. Constitutionally this decision was, in the early modern period, unproblematic. The monarch only needed to call a Parliament if he or she wanted to levy taxation. Other governmental instruments were available for the promulgation of laws. Charles could and did use the standing high court and council of Star Chamber to promulgate orders that had the force of law and that did not require Parliamentary endorsement. That mechanism was used, for example, to refine the measures for the control of dissident press activity.[2]

In the mid-1630s the personal rule of Charles I, as this period of government without Parliaments is often termed, was sailing relatively untroubled waters. The fiscal shortfall between the money the King could raise from his own fortunes and the money he needed to govern was being met by various measures of perhaps dubious legality, but there was a distinct sense that the regime was getting away with the rather authoritarian policy it had adopted. Church issues were potentially troublesome, however.[3]

The Caroline Church

From the time of the Elizabethan period, there had been radical English Protestants who would not accept the settlement of the church into an episcopalian and rather ceremonial form. The church was organized, much as it had been during its Catholic period, into dioceses governed by bishops through a hierarchy of senior clergy; the bishops reported in turn to the archbishops of York and Canterbury. The head of the church was the monarch, and the monarch had ultimate responsibility for appointing bishops and archbishops. Again, the order of church service, although in English, retained some of the features of the Catholic mass, and the general style of worship was heavily liturgical. From the Elizabethan period, the more extreme radicals separated from the state church (a dangerous policy in a country that enforced religious conformity and observance with the law). Many of these separatists, or Brownists as they were termed (after Robert Browne, an early leader), chose exile in Protestant parts of Continental Europe or, a little later, in the American settlements. Meanwhile, more moderate elements, still critical of episcopalian church government and of the liturgical nature of worship, sought to reform the church from within. The most influential group within this movement were the Presbyterians, who argued that the church should be governed from the bottom up by a system of committees, rather than from the top down through the hierarchy of senior clergy. The term "Puritanism," originally a term of abuse, can be applied both to the separatists (the future "Independents") and to those who, like the Presbyterians, remained within the Anglican communion.

Charles I was profoundly antipathetic to all manifestations of Puritanism. In the secular government of the realm, he had established a new ceremonial order on the conduct of his court, and he had shown a personal dislike of criticism and adverse comment. A sense of hierarchy and of the transcendence of the monarch is central to the informing political philosophy of the personal rule. Charles I's personal preferences in religious practices were, unsurprisingly, toward the ceremonial, and he was as intolerant of dissidents within the church as he was within the state. His principal instrument in refashioning the church to the monolithic and ceremonial standard he sought was William Laud, from 1633 archbishop of Canterbury, although a close associate of the King from early in his reign.

Laud's was a proactive style of ecclesiastical management. He secured the preferment of ministers who shared his and Charles I's values and assumptions. He elevated the status (and income) of the clergy. He began a program of church refurbishment (most significantly, at St. Paul's Cathedral, in the see of London, which he had held before promotion to Canterbury). He insisted on the scrupulous observation of the liturgical requirements of the church, and he innovated by revising the role of the communion table: formerly, and in line with most Protestant churches, it had stood in the nave, oriented along the length of the church and open to both clergy and laity. Laud's innovation was to have the table (or "altar," as he preferred to call it) removed to a (usually elevated) part of the church, at the east end, turned across the aisle, and separated from the laity by altar rails. To Puritans, this change seemed redolent of Catholicism, and the name "altar" struck them as pagan. Moreover—and the symbolism is easy enough to interpret—the communion table's orientation, its elevation, and its separation all asserted the redefined relationship between clergy and laity. Thus, even when matters were progressing well for Charles I and for Laud, church government and liturgical practices were feeding resentment among Anglicans and offending some who would not perhaps have originally thought of themselves as Puritan or oppositional.

Two other aspects of religion need to be discussed. Charles I was widely viewed as soft on Catholicism. He had, in Henrietta Maria, a devoutly Catholic queen, whose marriage settlement had required that she be allowed her own Catholic chapel, which in turn had become something of a focus for the residual Catholic minority among the English aristocracy. Occasional high-profile conversions to Catholicism caused alarm within some sections of an English population that was generally fiercely Protestant. Again, some aspects of the emphasis on church ceremony also smacked of a leaning to Rome. Historians currently disagree about the divisiveness of the doctrinal debates of the 1620s and 1630s. But certainly in that period some divines, who enjoyed the protection of the court, expounded a theory of salvation that ran counter to the hitherto almost unchallenged orthodoxies of Calvinism. Calvinism argued that God had predestined individuals to salvation and (in the extreme form of the doctrine) to damnation. The individual could do nothing by way of spiritual exercise or good works to influence the destination of his or her soul, although those who were saved manifested that salvation through the godliness of their conduct. In the Netherlands at the start of the seventeenth century, the Protestant church was riven by an alternative view expounded by Jacobus Arminius and his followers. In this doctrine, central to "Arminianism," God returned to individuals some of the free will that Adam and Eve lost at their fall; this free will then allowed individuals to choose to cooperate with the working of grace or the holy spirit within them to effect, through a process of synergy, their spiritual regeneration and salvation. It is altogether likely that most intellectually active Anglicans, whether of Puritanical orientation or not, opposed this newer doctrine, retaining a broad Calvinist consensus. According to Nicholas Tyacke, the Arminian innovation was a factor precipitating a crisis within the Caroline church.[4] Other historians, however, regard the issue as overstated; Laud and Charles were not really Arminians nor even that sympathetic to Arminians.[5] Certainly, "Arminianism," as a term of abuse if not as the denotation of precisely defined doctrinal position, was a charge laid against the leaders of the Caroline church by their opponents. Perhaps through a process of guilt by association, Arminianism was often confused with Catholicism, from which it certainly does not derive. Possibly its extension of the possibility of salvation to all fallen humankind seemed closer to the corresponding Catholic doctrine.

Beginnings of Opposition

Two crises deeply shook the otherwise assured progress of the personal rule and profoundly shaped the direction of Milton's life and career. The first came in 1637. Three leading Puritans, Henry Burton, John Bastwick, and William Prynne, were brought before the Star Chamber, charged with publishing tracts that defamed episcopacy. All three were seasoned campaigners, and Prynne was already in prison for publishing a Puritan attack on theaters that had scandalized the queen (for which he had already been mutilated by ear cropping). The three men were sentenced to mutilation at the pillory and to life imprisonment. Kevin Sharpe provides the fullest modern account, and he notes the uncooperativeness of the accused, whose conduct courted and secured their martyrdom; a more humble or conciliatory approach might well have found mercy.[6] Their strategy was one of extraordinary courage, and with courage did they discharge it. They spoke with great eloquence from the scaffold and endured their mutilation (in Prynne's case of the residual stumps of his ears) heroically:

> though [the executioner charged with the job] cut it deep and close to the head in an extraordinary manner yet this champion never moved nor stirred for it, and the temples and head arteries being cut so as the blood came streaming down on the scaffold which divers persons standing about the pillory dipped their handkerchiefs in as in a thing most precious, the people giving a mournful shout and a compassionate crying for the chirugeon {surgeon} whom the crowd and other impediments for a time kept off, that he could not come to staunch the stream of the blood, this patient all the while held his peace, holding up his hands and said be content, it is well, blessed be God.[7]

The crowd was moved by such fortitude.

Punishment in the early modern period often had such a spectacular element. The state sought to punish malefactors and to make that punishment witnessed by the population. There is a grisly symbolism in such mutilation, as in the hanging, drawing, and quartering of "traitors"; of the gibbeting of heads and limbs in prominent places, such as the gatehouse on London Bridge; or in public flagellation and exposure to ridicule in the pillory. The meaning is easy to read: the state is all-powerful and may do pretty much as it wishes with deviant elements, rendering them ludicrous, rendering them as creatures less than fully human, even dissolving their physical integrity and redistributing it at will.

Propertied Londoners like Milton, although perhaps locally critical of aspects of government (we simply have no evidence either way in his case), may well have felt that the legal apparatuses of the state substantially served their interest. Disorder threatened property, and they could only lose from civil unrest. But Prynne, Burton, and Bastwick were men like themselves. They were educated; they belonged to the learned professions of the church, the law, and medicine. In punishing them and in subjecting them to the kind of spectacular disgrace reserved for malefactors, the state was saying to Milton and his kind that they, too, were as powerless and unimportant as a common pickpocket or prostitute or clandestine Catholic priest. Educated men such as Milton may have thought that they were in an ordered society, that they were part of the hierarchy; in the bleeding stumps of the martyrs' ears, they could read the truth of their real relationship to the Caroline state.

It was in 1637, after the punishment of Prynne, Burton, and Bastwick, that Milton wrote, in understandably guarded terms, his first unequivocally Puritan text, the pastoral elegy "Lycidas." Shortly afterward, he left for a protracted stay in continental Europe. John T. Shawcross has sagely and convincingly argued that his family may have hastened him out of the way so he could not get into any political trouble.[8] I suspect that in these events we have the awakening of the revolutionary consciousness we encounter in 1641 in his first controversial prose works.

A second event accelerated the unraveling of the personal rule of Charles I: opposition from the citizens of his Scottish kingdom, at that time, of course, separate from England, with its own church and Parliament. Once more, the overconfidence of the Stuart state played its part as the King's attempts to reform Scottish religious practice along English lines precipitated conflict. That conflict led to armed resistance; twice Charles mustered armies to march north on what proved to be wholly abortive expeditions. But Charles was now picking up the kind of serious expense that he and his father had usually managed to avoid in the first four decades of the century. That expense could only be met by the levying of a kind of taxation that required the approval of Parliament. The Long Parliament, called in 1640, spilled out the pent-up opposition of decades of silence; William Laud was eventually arrested and imprisoned, along with Charles I's able first minister, the Earl of Wentworth (both subsequently to be decapitated); and political conflict so exasperated Charles that he withdrew from London and mustered his troops to suppress Parliament by force. In the summer of 1642, the Civil War began.

John Morrill argues that matters of religion drove the opponents of Charles into the course of action that precipitated the armed conflict:

> in the hectic early days of the Long Parliament, there were three quite distinct and separable perceptions of misgovernment or modes of opposition—what will be called the *localist,* the *legal-constitutionalist,* and the *religious*. One man could hold two or three of them; but many did not do so. . . . the localist and the legal-constitutionalist perceptions of misgovernment lacked the momentum, the passion, to bring about the kind of civil war which England experienced after 1642. It was the force of religion that drove minorities to fight, and forced majorities to make reluctant choices.[9]

Certainly in the period between the calling of the Long Parliament and the outbreak of the war, Milton did what he could to incense a reading public in implacable fashion against Caroline church government. The man who perhaps had left for Europe a fledgling revolutionary returned an accomplished champion of the revolutionary cause.

Two further points remain before we examine in turn each of Milton's tracts. At the time that Milton wrote these tracts, the outcome of the opposition to royal policy was very uncertain; the grisly fate of Bastwick, Burton, and Prynne may well have awaited the activists of 1640–1642. Second, Milton's tracts were contributions to current controversies. He was engaging what apologists of prelacy had written, and he was coming rather late to the debate (we don't know why he published nothing before May 1641). Rather like those earlier prolusions, these tracts were inserted into a debate the disposition of which was not in Milton's control.

Of Reformation

A group of Puritan divines, whose initials spelled the acronym SMECTYM-NUUS[10] under which they wrote, were locked in controversy with Bishop Joseph Hall by 1641. Hall was among the most talented writers on the royalist side. As a young man in Elizabethan London, he had been an accomplished and rather sensational creative writer, one of whose books was so risqué that it had been ordered to be burned by the hangman (a fact Milton recalled and used against him). More recently, because of his talent and because he was relatively uncontaminated by association with Laud, he had been promoted from the see of Exeter to the more lucrative see of Norwich. Most gallingly, he could write rather well. In his *Humble Remonstrance to the High Court of Parliament,* published in late December or early January (the title page says "1640"), he argued that the major issues dividing the church were not that significant; that there was a good consensus about what really mattered; and that politically motivated men, "furious and malignant spirits,"[11] were exploiting a technical discussion in order to provoke tumult and disorder. Hall gratingly hits a consistent tone of elevated assurance, which he maintains throughout the debate.

Smectymnuus responded in March 1641[12] with *An Answer to a Booke Entituled, An Humble Remonstrance,* a longer and tediously verbose refutation that surely no one could have read then or since with interest or pleasure. Hall answered it with *A Defence of the Humble Remonstrance* (April 1641), hitting a singularly patronizing tone toward his junior ecclesiastical colleagues, his "younger brethren." Smectymnuus lobbed an even heavier response, *A Vindication of the Answer to the Humble Remonstrance* (June 1641). In July Hall issued his *Short Answer to the Tedious Vindication of Smectymnuus.* This was the milieu of response and counterresponse into which Milton inserted himself.

Milton's first pamphlet, *Of Reformation touching Church-Discipline in England and the Causes that hitherto have hindred it,* appeared anonymously in May 1641. Although the war of words between Hall and Smectymnuus remained very active, in fact by that date the campaign by Puritans seeking a more radical reformation of the church of England was losing some of its urgency. Indeed, while Smectymnuus and Hall were trading insults, it is quite possible that some of the former were in secret negotiation with Hall and his *confrères* to explore ways of botching together a compromise that would have made the style of the church acceptable to Puritans while retaining bishops. A little earlier there had been a monster petition for the "root-and-branch" reform of the church, and undoubtedly that was what Milton sought; but the campaign had lost direction. I rather suspect it was Milton's sense of this dangerous drift toward compromise, rather than any pressing personal loyalty to a member of the Smectymnuan writing team, that prompted Milton to pitch in.

His own tract is utterly implacable toward the bishops. It ends with an extraordinary vision of what will happen once Christ returns to earth to judge the quick and the dead, an event that Milton, like many others at that time, evidently thought could be imminent. There is a millenarian optimism in his anticipation of the thousand-year rule on earth of saints like himself, the godly who will be incorporated into Christ's happy band. At that day "the Eternall and shortly-expected King" shall "open the Clouds to judge the severall Kingdomes of the World." Then,

> they undoubtedly that by their *Labours, Counsels,* and *Prayers* have been earnest for the *Common good* of *Religion* and their *Countrey,* shall . . . clasp inseparable Hands with *joy,* and *blisse* in over measure for ever.

He means, of course, those Puritan activists who have struggled for the reformation of the English church (although this is a vision of the end of the world, Milton's focus seems to rest rather narrowly on England). A rather different fate awaits the bishops:

> But they contrary that by the impairing and diminution of the true *Faith,* the distresses and servitude of their *Countrey* aspire to high *Dignity, Rule* and *Promotion* here, after a shamefull end in this *Life* (which *God* grant them) shall be thrown downe eternally into the *darkest* and *deepest Gulfe* of HELL, where under the *despightfull controule,* the trample and spurne of all the other *Damned,* that in the anguish of their *Torture* shall have no other ease then to exercise a *Raving* and *Bestiall Tyranny* over them as their *Slaves* and *Negro's,* they shall remaine in that plight for ever,

the *basest,* the *lowermost,* the *most dejected,* most *underfoot* and *downe-trodden Vassals of Perdition.* (*CPW*, I, 616–17)

The violence of this "vision" cannot be mistaken. But we should note that it extends to the immediate temporal fate of the bishops as well as to their eternal damnation. "After a shamefull end in this *Life* (which *God* grant them)" is probably a call for their execution. Laud's arrest had occurred in the month before the publication of *Of Reformation;* other bishops were impeached in mid-1641 and by the end of the year were charged with high treason (though never subsequently convicted of the charge).[13] High treason carried the death penalty, usually by hanging, drawing, and quartering, the most "shamefull" death England had devised in the early modern period. Parliament was too busy running the war to deal with Laud then and there, but early in 1645 he was brought to trial and found guilty. By this time, the years of war had made the vindictive act generally popular with a broad spectrum of Puritan opinion, although it can scarcely be surprising that the twice-docked Prynne led the prosecution. Hanging was commuted to decapitation as a merciful gesture.

So Milton's gleeful fantasy, although it may have anticipated events to some extent and although it extended to *all* bishops the fate that was to be Laud's alone, is not radically out of line with contemporary Puritian opinion, even though it is on the extreme edge of that ideology. There is no reason to doubt the sincerity of his conclusion, worked out through the huge sentences that end that tract, like a consummation labored for and achieved by the godly and by God. But Milton, even in his earliest tract, recalls the polemical guile instilled by a traditional education in rhetoric. What he does is equate all bishops and damn them all with the worst excesses of the few, and he extends the equation to the whole ecclesiastical history of England.

Of course, maintaining the argument requires a certain boldness. He caps a series of historical anecdotes demonstrating how bishops have undermined the monarchy in England thus:

What good upholders of Royalty were the *Bishops,* when by their rebellious opposition against King *John, Normandy* was lost, he himselfe depos'd, and this Kingdome made over to the *Pope?* When the *Bishop* of *Winchester* durst tell the Nobles, the Pillars of the Realme, that there were no Peeres in *England,* as in *France,* but that the King might doe what hee pleas'd. What could Tyranny say more? it would bee petty now if I should insist upon the rendring up of *Tournay* by *Woolseyes* Treason, the

> Excommunications, Cursings, and Interdicts upon the whole Land. For
> haply I shall be cut off short by a reply, that these were the faults of the
> men, and their Popish errors, not of *Episcopacie,* that hath now renounc't
> the Pope, and is a Protestant. Yes sure; as wise and famous men have sus-
> pected, and fear'd the Protestant *Episcopacie* in *England,* as those that have
> fear'd the Papall. (*CPW,* I, 581)

Milton half-concedes the fallacy of his case, but drives on with the accu-
mulation of historical anecdote, as if weaving pre- and post-Reformation
episcopal conduct into a seamless garment of infamy. He develops a
powerful binary opposition between the simplicities and clarities of
Christian religion, as inscribed in the gospel, and the ugly accretions of
prelatical tradition. The Puritan case is that church government on the
prelatical model is not of apostolic origin, but rather was added to the
church as, in subsequent ages, it became corrupt and its leaders sought
personal aggrandizement. Later traditions of interpretation, associated
with the divines of the subsequent centuries, the Church Fathers, have
their justification in the supposed obscurity of the gospel; but what the
Christian really needs to know is plain enough: "The very essence of
Truth is plainnesse, and brightnes; the darknes and crookednesse is our
own" (*CPW,* I, 566).

That sentiment is characteristic of a feature of this tract: the way in
which the argument is often carried, not by logical exposition, but by a
driving Puritan aesthetic that values plainness and purity and depre-
cates adornment as something vile and excrescent. It simultaneously, in
a sort of subliminal way, equates traditional or patristic interpretative
additions to the gospel with additions to the pristine structure of the
primitive church. Episcopacy is like a great "Wen" or wart, "a heape of
hard, and loathsome uncleannes . . . a foul disfigurment and burden"
(*CPW,* I, 583–84). Bishops are "the Ulcers of the Kingdome," which
draw resources from its veins by their extortions and corruptions (*CPW,*
I, 590–91). Or else that primitive purity is like an honest woman now
decked in the garments of a prostitute:

> the *Prelates* . . . comming from a meane, and Plebeyan *Life* on a sudden to
> be Lords of stately Palaces, rich furniture, delicious fare, and *Princely*
> attendance, thought the plaine and homespun verity of *Christs* Gospell
> unfit any longer to hold their Lordships acquaintance, unlesse the poore
> thred-bare Matron were put into better clothes; her chast and modest
> vaile surrounded with celestiall beames they overlai'd with wanton *tresses,*

and in a flaring tire bespecckl'd her with all the gaudy allurements of a Whore. (*CPW*, I, 556–57)

The passage is suffused with characteristically Puritan values. It reflects a sense that prelacy manifests conspicuous indulgence and that bishops have used the hierarchical structure of church government to advance themselves from lowly to princely positions at the expense of the middle sort of people for whom and to whom Milton speaks. There is, too, a horror at sexual libertinism, in contrast with the valorization, in women, of a humble, honest plainness.

Milton knows how to tug a Puritan's strings, and he knows it so well because he probably shares those values and assumptions. For such a cerebral writer, he seems surprisingly uninterested in the theoretical arguments against prelacy and against the Laudian government of the church. Nowhere in this tract does he take issue with matters of doctrine, that is, of belief, that may have divided Puritan from Laudian. He shows an obvious impatience with the whole body of patristic commentary (something to which we shall return in consideration of his later antiprelatical tracts). The issue of Arminianism, to which Tyacke attributes such a cardinal significance, simply is not engaged by Milton (whether because it was generally less a factor in the crisis than Tyacke suggests, or because Milton is not animated by that doctrinal matter).[14] Indeed, he explicitly remarks that discipline (that is, how the church is run, its ceremonies, its church government), not doctrine, separates the Church of England from Continental reformed churches, paradigmatically the Church of Geneva, of which English Puritans approve and which they take as the model for their own current second reformation in England: "in *purity* of *Doctrine* we agree with our [Continental] Brethren; yet in Discipline . . . we are no better then a *Schisme,* from all the *Reformation,* and a sore scandall to them" (*CPW*, I, 526).

Milton's focus falls persistently on excrescent practices, on the unnecessary vestments not required in the gospel, on the orientation of altar as a separation of the laity from the clergy, on the practice of making the sign of the cross, on the liturgy based on an Anglican adaptation of the mass book it superseded, indeed on all "those sencelesse *Ceremonies* which wee onely retaine, as a dangerous earnest of sliding back to *Rome*" (*CPW*, I, 526–27). His own apparent horror of Catholicism appears frequently enough throughout his mature writings, both poetry and prose, but in incorporating it into his attack on the bishops, he follows a strategy almost universally adopted among Puritan writers and one well capable of tainting the episcopalian position.

Who is the target audience for *Of Reformation?* Whom does he want to persuade, and of what? The last, I think, is there to be recognized in the text: he wants to carry the notion that prelacy is a tradition so unacceptable to the true Christian faith and so hostile to the godly down the centuries that it cannot be tolerated even in revised form. The audience must be a broad spectrum of Puritan belief, both those who share his root-and-branch enthusiasm for extirpating prelacy and those whose initial zeal is giving way to a search for a less destructive middle way.

Milton, as a principal mode of capturing the good will of his intended readers, produces within the tract an image of himself constructed to that end. He parades his own Puritan values (hence that oblique praise of the honest Puritan matron). And he offers himself as a friend and guide through the seeming complexities of the issues, presenting them instead as really rather simple, a choice between the plainness of the gospel truths and the mind-numbing patristic pseudo-scholarship of the prelates.

Of Prelatical Episcopacy

A similar strategy informs his second pamphlet, *Of Prelatical Episcopacy, and Whether it may be deduc'd from the Apostolical times by vertue of those Testimonies which are alledg'd to that purpose in some late Treatises: One whereof goes under the Name of Iames Arch-bishop of Armagh,* first published in June or July 1641.

As the title suggests, this tract is directly and immediately controversial, attacking a tract by James Ussher. The archbishop of Armagh was the most senior Protestant clergyman in Charles's kingdom of Ireland— of itself, perhaps, no remarkable position, because then, as now, Catholicism was the majority religion across the whole island, and most Protestants were Presbyterians. But his status rested, too, on his scholarship. As one surveys the British intellectual landscape in the 1640s, probably only two figures of genuinely international standing emerge. One was the polymath John Selden, who was a Parliamentary supporter. The other was James Ussher. Nowadays he is most often recalled (usually facetiously) as the man who dated the foundation of the world at 4004 B.C. What is forgotten is that in his own age he was admired as a scholar who had ingeniously correlated biblical events with world history. He was an antiquarian and biblical scholar of the first order. Hall had wheeled him into action to establish, by invoking the early history of the church, that bishops had been of apostolic institution, a point Ussher had sustained in a pamphlet issued in May 1641 to counter an Elizabethan pamphlet that antiprelatical activists had reissued earlier in the year. But his was but one of a cluster of antiquarian justifications of prelacy that rested on the evidence of the church fathers.[15]

Of Prelatical Episcopacy is a scintillating little tract of some 24 pages, a Puritan's guide to why one need not worry about patristic evidence. Laud had been an eager promoter of a revived interest in the writings of the Greek church fathers since his days as chancellor of the university of Oxford, and lately it has been argued that this educational initiative was central to the cultural revolution he effected within the Church of England.[16] Milton avoids tackling his principal opponent directly— Ussher was a heavyweight scholar above his division—nor does he really sift and evaluate each piece of evidence relating to the early history of the Christian church. His is altogether a brisker method.

Two principles, by his own account, shape the survival of ancient records. The first is sheer luck:

> Whatsoever time, or the heedlesse hand of blind chance, hath drawne down from of old to this present, in her huge dragnet, whether Fish, or Sea-weed, Shells, or Shrubbs, unpickt, unchosen, those are the Fathers. (*CPW*, I, 626)

What survives is so much flotsam on the beach of time. But Milton is too shrewd to leave the argument at that point. A second principle obtains: whatever survives has been preserved and transmitted by the Catholic tradition of scholarship. Thus, *The Acts of Timothy*, attributed to Polycrates, is "sent us from the shop of the Jesuites at *Lovain*" (*CPW*, I, 633), so Ussher's scholarship on that point is based on something tainted with Catholicism.

What has come down may indeed contain real evidence, but the record is corrupted, not only by tendentious editing and the hand of time, but also by the heresies and superstitions of the postapostolic age. Alongside the sometimes valid comments of church fathers are heresies, which must mean either that the surviving documentation was subsequently corrupted (which could apply to any part of it) or else that these fathers were themselves manifesting a falling off from the doctrinal purity of the apostles. Milton is also contemptuous of that hagiographical tradition that trades on miraculous anecdotes. Thus people who had actually met the apostles were esteemed beyond their real moral status; fantastic stories spread ("that pavement bedew'd with the warme effusion of his [a martyr's] last blood, that sprouted up into eternall Roses to crowne his Martyrdome"—*CPW,* I, 642); and the simple purity of the gospel text was ignored.

As in *Of Reformation, Of Prelatical Episcopacy* presents a straightforward opposition of the gospel—the text that is divinely validated—and human tradition, Scripture "being the onely Book left us of *Divine* authority, not in any thing more Divine then in the all-sufficiency it hath" to resolve the question of church government (*CPW,* I, 625). Reassuringly, one does not need to read the *patrologia* in order to resolve the matter. From an early date, Milton's polemic often has a surprisingly robust and perhaps even anti-intellectual populism, at least at the level of argument, although the exposition is characteristically demanding of its reader.

Yet *Of Prelatical Episcopacy* is, by Miltonic standards, a polite text. The nature of the argument he was entering resembled academic discourse, with its usual courtesies, and anyway Ussher deserved respect. (When the Puritans in Parliament set up a grand conference, called the Westminster Assembly of Divines, to review doctrine, Ussher was one of the few episcopalians invited to attend, although he declined.)[17] Indeed, Milton behaves as though the debate is still within a state church; whatever we may think of bishops and of the antiquaries who argue for their institutional survival, they are all still English Protestants, "our men" (*CPW,* I, 651). In his next pamphlet, a rather different tone emerges.

Animadversions

The title indicates the maturity of the debate and Milton's point of intercession: this pamphlet is *Animadversions upon The Remonstrants Defence against Smectymnuus,* Milton's comments on Joseph Hall's comments on Smectymnuus's comments on Hall's *Humble Remonstrance.* Hall had published in April 1641; Milton responded probably in July.[18]

His pamphlet certainly owes something to the Cambridge of his youth. Like some of his *Prolusions,* this tract is utterly and closely combative, and it displays a scabrous wit. It has, too, some of the qualities of a duel (not for the last time in his prose oeuvre). The debate is deeply personalized, and Milton juxtaposes a self-image of a Puritan zealot, who is nevertheless witty and sometimes risqué, with an image of Hall as an effete roué and supercilious poseur.

The format of the pamphlet is simple. Milton quotes a passage from Hall's attack on Smectymnuus, and then caps it brutally:

Remonstr. [i.e., the
Remonstrant, Hall]   They [Smectymnuus] cannot name any man in
                       this Nation that ever contradicted *Episcopacie,* till
                       this present Age.

Answ. [i.e., Milton]   What an over-worne and bedrid Argument is
                       this, the last refuge ever of old falshood, and
                       therefore a good signe I trust that your Castle
                       cannot hold out long. This was the plea of
                       Judaisme, and Idolatry against *Christ* and his *Apos-
                       tles,* of *Papacie* against Reformation. (*CPW,* I, 703)

Once more, of course, Milton plays the popery card: Hall's response to those Puritans demanding the second reformation parallels Catholicism's response to Luther, that he challenged an institution that previously was unchallenged.

As if suspecting that a tract that works virtually paragraph by paragraph through somebody's response to somebody else's comments on somebody's statements has the potential to seem stale, Milton aims to strike a jaunty and witty tone. As his preface rather pompously puts it,

> *in the serious uncasing of a grand imposture (for to deale plainly with you Read-
> ers, Prelatry is no better) there be mixt here and there such a grim laughter, as
> may appear at the same time in an austere visage, it cannot be taxt of levity or
> insolence.* (*CPW,* I, 663)

I rather suspect here a preemptive gesture by a young writer who perhaps felt he had gone too far. "Grim laughter" sometimes has a rather boyish air:

Remon.   No one Clergie in the whole Christian world
             yeelds so many eminent schollers, learned
             preachers, grave, holy and accomplish'd Divines
             as this Church of *England* doth at this day.

Answ.   Ha, ha, ha. (*CPW,* I, 726)

Yet there is nevertheless a sustained argument developed in *Animadversions,* one that synthesizes the root-and-branch argumentation in *Of
Reformation* with the impatience with tradition articulated in *Of Prelatical*

Episcopacy. With a grotesque flourish, Milton characterizes those who would make the church a lucrative profession in which to place their sons as "wretched Fathers" anxious to advance "their sordid sperm begotten in the lustinesse of their avarice" and "that lump of flesh which they are the cause of" (*CPW,* I, 722). Milton recognizes the shifts in power within the state that have left the Puritans in a position to treat bishops much as bishops once treated Puritans. Hall, perhaps unwisely, ponders whether Smectymnuus may be open to prosecution; Milton responds,

> The punishing of that which you call our presumption and disobedience lies not now within the execution of your fangs, the mercifull God above and our just Parliament will deliver us from your *Ephesian* beasts, your cruell *Nimrods,* with whom we shall be ever fearelesse to encounter. (*CPW,* I, 729)

We are the masters now, Milton reflects; the bishops themselves may soon receive appropriate punishment "for the lopping, and stigmatizing [i.e., branding] of so many free borne Christians" (*CPW,* I, 728).

The old bugbear, Tradition, returns as a figure of ghastly gigantism. The arguments from antiquity are a vast statue, impressive in bulk but somewhat exposed to the defecation of birds:

> Why doe wee therefore stand worshipping, and admiring this unactive, and livelesse *Colossus,* that like a carved Gyant terribly menacing to children, and weaklings lifts up his club, but strikes not, and is subject to the muting of every Sparrow. If you let him rest upon his *Basis,* hee may perhaps delight the eyes of some with his huge and mountainous Bulk, and the quaint workmanship of his massie limbs; but if yee goe about to take him in pieces, yee marre him. (*CPW,* I, 699)

According to Milton, arguments from antiquity share the grossness of pagan state art on a gigantic scale, and there are those that would worship it as pagans worship idols. In Milton's now familiar contrast, argument from scripture has clarity, purity, and divine sanction; it functions to topple those pagan idols:

> Wee shall adhere close to the Scriptures of God which hee hath left us as the just and adequate measure of truth, fitted, and proportion'd to the diligent study, memory, and use of every faithfull man . . . with this

> weapon . . . wee shall not doubt to batter, and throw down your *Neb-uchadnezzars* Image and crumble it like the chaffe of the Summer thresh-ing floores . . . (*CPW,* I, 700)

The toppling of the icons of the displaced regime is as much a feature of our own age as of Milton's.

A new issue, however, emerges in this tract, and one that points to incipient divisions within the Puritan camp that, within months, would break open the uneasy alliances of 1640–1642. Presbyterians, such as members of the Smectymnuus team, shared with episcopalians a com-mitment to the notion of a state church that should embrace all English people and that should enforce uniformity of belief and worship. What Presbyterians wanted was a second reformation, to bring the Church of England into alignment with, for example, the Church of Geneva that Calvin had founded. Thereafter, they supported measures to control unorthodox beliefs and to ensure that clergy worshipped according to a (reformed) liturgical pattern.

But there were other opinions on the issue of uniformity. Some Puri-tan divines argued that different congregations should be free to develop their own styles of worship and their own doctrinal positions, and that each Christian should be allowed to select among those congregations to find a style and a doctrine to which he or she could in conscience sub-scribe. This more tolerationist position—variously termed Indepen-dency or congregationalism or congregational Independency—had developed among Puritan emigrés in the American settlements, some of whom returned to London in the upsurge of optimism of the very early 1640s. But tolerationism often meant tolerance of a wide spectrum of sometimes rather eccentric beliefs and practices.

For besides the solid middle ground of Puritan opinion, sects rapidly developed and achieved an almost instant notoriety. They had a long ancestry among heretical groups both in England and in continental Europe, and their most spectacular precursors (or so their enemies claimed) were the Anabaptists who had established a bizarre rule of the saints in Münster in the 1540s. This group, whom Luther had opposed and who were eventually suppressed by the Elector of Saxony with spec-tacular brutality, had taken over the city and seemingly held property and women in common (their history is told, of course, only by their vic-tors). That regime, apparently led for the most part by men of little or no property, offered a vivid example of the disorders possible once the constraints of a state religion are cast off.

Münsterian Anabaptists, besides disputing the validity of baptizing infants into the Christian faith, were also, apparently, antinomians. That is, they believed that the force of the Mosaic law of the Ten Commandments was suspended in their case because they had within them the Holy Spirit. So the old constraints protecting property and forbidding promiscuity no longer applied. What this brand of Anabaptism shares with many of the more extreme groups is an ancient heresy that suggests that the Trinity of Father, Son, and Holy Ghost functions chronologically rather than simultaneously: Old Testament times, when the law was handed to Moses, was the age of the Father; when Christ was on earth, his word had authority; but now is the age of the Spirit, of a godhead internalized within each believer. That believer is as pure as Adam had been before the fall and need feel no shame about his or her nakedness; he or she is sinless and cannot sin, even by doing things that in the eyes of the world are held sinful (such as group sex).

A class aspect rapidly emerged. The leaders of the Münsterians had come from outside the traditional propertied classes that made up the hierarchy supporting states in the early modern period. Similarly, the leaders of these more extreme groups or sects in and around London were not professional clergy and were often (as their enemies stressed) members of the trades class, people of little property and no education.

Just as antiprelatical propaganda frequently accused bishops of tolerating or encouraging or even being more or less Catholics, so anti-Puritan propaganda accused Puritans either of being or encouraging sectaries. This tactic has found a place in two game plans: it is a charge leveled by episcopalians against Presbyterians in 1640–1642, and it is used from about 1642 onward by moderate Puritans, such as Presbyterians, to besmirch Independents and tolerationists.

Milton's first involvement with the issues is wholly defensive. To the charge that the moderate Puritanism now dominant in church and Parliament fosters the sects, Milton replies in *Animadversions* that heterodoxy is not easy to control and that historically episcopalian church government had a poor record of controlling it. Heresy was endemic within the early episcopalian church, and its various councils and edicts, although they give evidence of the extent of the problem, could not control it (*CPW*, I, 685). In his next tract, Milton moves much closer to the issue.

The Reason of Church-Government

The Reason of Church-Governement Urg'd against Prelaty By Mr. John Milton was probably first published early in 1642 (although the title page has "1641") and was intended as a refutation of a collection of essays by several episcopalian hands, perhaps edited by Archbishop Ussher, entitled *Certain Briefe Treatises, Written by Diverse Learned Men, Concerning the Ancient and Moderne Government of the Church* (Oxford, 1641).[19] For the first time, Milton's name actually appears on the title page, and as we shall see, this pamphlet is a surprisingly intimate self-presentation by the author. But striking, too, is the sudden confusion about how the sects are to be regarded.

Although Milton had touched earlier on the issue of sects, it had not previously been a major concern. As I have remarked elsewhere,[20] the words "sect(s)," "sectaries," "schism(s)" and "schismatic(s)" (virtual synonyms for sects and sectaries) occur only 6 times in Milton's first three pamphlets, but occur 70 times in *The Reason of Church-Government,* in which he returns almost neurotically to the issue.

What he has to say about the sects does not really hold together. In *Animadversions* he had played to the moderate Puritan agenda, not disputing the undesirability of sects but arguing that episcopacy was no more effective than any other form of church government at controlling their spread. In *The Reason of Church-Government,* we still encounter that argument. In the postapostolic episcopalian church, "Heresie begat heresie with a certain monstrous haste of pregnancy in her birth, at once borne and bringing forth" (*CPW,* I, 781). At the same time, he argues that the other side exaggerates how big a problem the emergent sects constitute. They are "partly the meere fictions and false alarmes of the Prelates, thereby to cast amazements and panick terrors into the hearts of weaker Christians," rumors spread to pressure people into accepting episcopacy lest by displacing it they admit sectaries with all their concomitant threats to social order and property (*CPW,* I, 794). These arguments are not suggesting that sects are not a nuisance, only that they are a minor one that need not deflect the godly from that secondary reformation currently under way: "If God come to trie our constancy we ought not to shrink, or stand the lesse firmly for that, but passe on with more stedfast resolution to establish the truth though it were through a lane of sects and heresies on each side" (*CPW,* I, 794–95). The great upheaval in which the Church of England was engaged must necessarily have produced a few wrong turns, a smattering of temporary errors. A great debate involved "the struggl of contrarieties" (*CPW,* I, 795); there were bound to be "many fond errors and fanatick opinions, which when truth has the upper hand, and the reformation shall be perfeted, will easily be rid out of the way, or kept so low, as that they shall be only the exercise of our knowledge, not the disturbance, or interruption of our faith" (*CPW,* I, 796).

So after the secondary reformation, the godly will either wipe out the sects or tolerate them as a kind of hobby. The godly will study them to note and distinguish their foibles. To the argument that prelacy is justified as a bulwark against the sects, Milton responds that the sects are not the main problem. But he is by no means always that hostile to heterodox opinion. Indeed, he rhapsodizes that the revived Church of England will be a church broad enough to readmit independent congregationalists, the heirs to the Brownists:

> Noise it till ye be hoarse; that a rabble of Sects will come in, it will be answer'd ye, no rabble sir Priest, but a unanimous multitude of good Protestants will then joyne to the Church, which now because of you stand separated. . . . As for those terrible names of Sectaries and Schismaticks which ye have got together, we know your manner of fight . . . whom ye could not move by sophisticall arguing, them you thinke to confute by scandalous misnaming. Thereby inciting the blinder sort of people to mislike and deride sound doctrine and good christianity under two or three vile and hatefull terms. . . . the Primitive Christians in their times were accounted such as are now call'd Familists and Adamites, or worse. (*CPW,* I, 787–88)

This complex passage poses some fascinating problems of interpretation and merits a close scrutiny. Who then are to be readmitted? Certainly the separatists, and that means primarily the congregational Independents. We shall shortly encounter Milton asserting yet again the merits of Presbyterianism—he is sure that no "wrincle or spot should be found in presbyterial government" (*CPW,* I, 834)—but he is evidently concerned that others outside that narrow pale have essential material to contribute to the Puritan reformation. The names are still "terrible," but they do not match the godliness of those who are traduced. He objects to the tactic of calling all unorthodox thinkers by the tainted terms historically applied to the strangest groups and those most dangerous to the social fabric, what he calls "scandalous misnaming." But a genuinely subversive logic is running here: the earliest Christians, living in a spirit of apostolic purity, were held in the same regard that those who are *now* called Familists and Adamites are *now* held. "Adamitism" was the heresy of going naked to demonstrate a purity equal to that before the fall. There probably was no "Adamite" sect in England in the mid-seventeenth century, but certainly radical sectaries did sometimes "go naked for a sign" and it was an element in early Quakerism.[21] The "Familists," also known as "the Family of Love," were a radical underground sect of almost legendary notoriety. The movement was founded by Henry Niclaes, a Münsterian, in the mid-sixteenth century. The sect seems to have been characterized by some of the utterly subversive impulses that found expression among the Münsterian Anabaptists:

> Familists believed that men and women might recapture on earth the state of innocence which existed before the Fall. . . . They held their property in common, believed that all things come by nature, and that only the spirit of God within the believer can properly understand Scripture.[22]

Milton's sense is not clear. He may be saying that early Christians were inaccurately traduced just as some are nowadays who are not Adamites and Familists. But the larger argument suggests that such a taxonomy of unacceptable belief has no place in revolutionary England.

Milton's shift to the tolerationist position marks a new uncertainty about matters of doctrine. He had had little to say about it thus far, focusing his antiprelatical attacks on external aspects of religious practice, on liturgy, on ceremonies, and on church government. But heresy is a matter of belief, not practice, and Milton's most resonant passages in this tract proclaim a cultural revolution in which a thousand flowers of heterodox thought may bloom. Thus, he remarks of the argument that episcopacy suppresses schism,

> The Winter might as well vaunt it selfe against the Spring, I destroy all noysome and rank weeds, I keepe downe all pestilent vapours. Yes and all wholesome herbs, and all fresh dews, by your violent & hidebound frost; but when the gentle west winds shall open the fruitfull bosome of the earth thus over-girded by your imprisonment, then the flowers put forth and spring, and then the Sunne shall scatter the mists, and the manuring hand of the Tiller shall root up all that burdens the soile without thank to your bondage. (*CPW,* I, 785)

This passage has two aspects. That image, of the weeds and good plants growing together until the reaping, echoes Christ's parable in which tares grow up among the corn until all are harvested (at the Last Judgment) (Matthew 13:24–30). The Puritan revolution need not hunt out its heretics, because at the imminent millennium Christ and his angels will perform the task. But the positive celebration of doctrinal diversity cannot be missed in the ideological *Primavera* in which "the fruitfull bosome of the earth" is opened. Here, a thriving life of the mind and the soul breaks open the frostbound earth with a vigor not to be resisted.

At the same time that Milton hails a new spring, a decided lassitude enters his own defense of the moderate Puritan position he has undertaken to support. At the heart of his now-familiar attacks on episcopacy comes a passage of self-revelation that exposes an almost embarrassing fragility. In the middle of this great debate, to which he has already contributed three pamphlets, he suddenly confesses himself sick of it all. He seems to know the risk of this autobiographical digression, to know how unusual it is in this kind of writing "to venture and divulge unusual things of my selfe" (*CPW,* I, 808). But he goes on, offering an image of himself as reluctant polemicist—prose, he says, is not really his medium, he writes it as if with his left hand. Rather, he is a cultured man of the Renaissance, a traveled man celebrated in the academies of Italy, a man who had thought it his destiny to write the English national epic. Now he must soak himself in grim antiquarian research to silence the prelatical apologists; he must leave the contemplative life and endure the ghastliness of polemical exchanges:

> I trust hereby to make it manifest with what small willingnesse I endure to interrupt the pursuit of no lesse hopes then these, and leave a calme and pleasing solitarines fed with cherful and confident thoughts, to imbark in a troubl'd sea of noises and hoars disputes, put from beholding the bright countenance of truth in the quiet and still air of delightfull studies. (*CPW,* I, 821–22)

A commitment to truth calls him to the battle, but there remains a distinct sense of wanting to be elsewhere. The noise and disputes come from all sides, not just from the bishops.

Although it is his longest tract to date, ideologically it is his most obscure. He knows the Presbyterian policy on sectaries, but he also feels an impulse toward tolerationism, a hope that all godly Protestants can live together in a transformed and more open Church of England, and a sense, too, that it does not much matter because "the Tiller" is shortly to gather up everyone, good plants and weeds, at a Last Judgment. Personally, he finds himself again cranking out the party line while longing for retreat and retirement, writing poems to "leave something so written to aftertimes, as they [Englishmen] should not willingly let it die" (*CPW,* I, 810), and contemplating, without constraint, the strange seas of thought on which he was shortly to embark. He had put himself at the heart of the tract and he had put his name on the title page; bewildered though he seems, his writing conveys a sense of a man approaching a point of decision.

An Apology

His last tract in the exchange is in some ways the simplest of this group, although its title shows that it contributes to a debate that has the ripeness of a Gorgonzola forgotten at the back of a refrigerator: *An Apology Against a Pamphlet call'd A Modest Confutation of the Animadversions upon the Remonstrant against* SMECTYMNUUS. This pamphlet answers an attack on his attack on Joseph Hall's attack on the Smectymnuan attack on Joseph Hall. It dates from the spring of 1642 and responds to an anonymous pamphlet called *A Modest Confutation of a Slanderous and Scurrilous Libell, Entituled, Animadversions etc.,* which had appeared a little earlier. It is usually thought that Hall's son may have written it, perhaps helped by his father.

The attack on Milton was so personal and so slighting that he had no option but to defend himself. Episcopalian apologists had been attacking Puritans in a satirical way since the Elizabethan period, usually implying their fanaticism, sometimes associating this fanaticism with a low cunning directed to the ends of personal ambition. What the Modest Confuter had done was to take the occasional hint from Milton's attack in *Animadversions* to build up a fantasy picture of a mean-minded hypocrite, looking to kick out good bishops to make room for himself. The Modest Confuter also pointed out that because Milton occasionally talks about brothels (usually in his imagery), he must be a man who knows his way around them, and so on.

Milton's answer serves to show how well he remembered the polemical games of his student days, and how effectively he can stoop to this discourse. A man who a few weeks earlier was longing for the poet's singing robes pulls on the pugilist's gloves to mete out a bit of condign punishment.

Thus it is that the professional episcopalian clergy in general and Hall in particular come in for Milton's ridicule and abuse. So the confuter thinks Milton knows his way to the brothel, does he? How well Milton remembers these future clergymen from his student days, as

they hammed it up in drag in student drama for the delectation of
depraved visiting courtiers, male and female:

> in the Colleges so many of the young Divines, and those in next aptitude
> to Divinity have bin seene so oft upon the Stage writhing and unboning
> their Clergie limmes to all the antick and dishonest gestures of Trin-
> culo's, Buffons, and Bawds; prostituting the shame of that ministery
> which either they had, or were nigh having, to the eyes of Courtiers and
> Court-Ladies, with their Groomes and *Madamoisellaes*. There while they
> acted, and overacted, among other young scholars, I was a spectator;
> they thought themselves gallant men, and I thought them fools, they
> made sport, and I laught, they mispronounc't and I mislik't, and . . .
> they were out, and I hist. (*CPW,* I, 887)

Milton the young Puritan sees undelighted all the thespian delight of
men who now preen themselves in their Laudian gravity. But the child,
for Milton, is the father of the man, and these men were fools when they
were fifteen and are fools now. They liked obscenities then, and secretly
they probably like them now. (Of course, we only have Milton's account
of his student days.)

This is a surprisingly easy game to play against Hall, for Hall in his
younger days was a rather risqué writer of satires that had been shock-
ing enough to have been burned. What would others think of Milton if
he had written like Hall used to write? "Surely he would have then concluded me as constant at the Bordello, as the gally-slave at his Oare?"
(*CPW,* I, 887). The *Apology,* necessarily reactive, lacks some of the glorious arrogance of *Animadversions,* although Milton demonstrates, not for
the last time, that in mid-century, polemic attack can be an effective
mode of defense.

Chapter Four

The Divorce Tracts, *Areopagitica,* and *Of Education*

[I]n 1969—just as the great waves of sexual liberation and radical life-style were breaking over the West—a bill was introduced into the House of Commons, by a back-bencher, Mr L. Abse, to convert this new idea of no-fault divorce into the law of the land. Abandoning the ancient principle of matrimonial fault, there was now to be substituted the principle, first enunciated back in the 1640s by John Milton, that the only just ground for divorce was as relief from the irremediable breakdown of a marital relationship. . . . the bill passed, to become law on 1 January 1971.

—Lawrence Stone, *Road to Divorce: England, 1530–1987*

In August 1643 Milton published the first edition of his first divorce tract, now usually referred to simply as *The Doctrine and Discipline of Divorce.* We shall return to its full title shortly. He had stopped publishing polemical prose some 16 months earlier, a decision perhaps reflecting disenchantment with the noisy scuffles of that genre that he had avowed in the autobiographical digression in *The Reason of Church-Government.*[1] But neither Milton nor the country had been idle. In August 1642 Charles I had raised military forces to suppress Parliament and recapture the government of England. Parliament had responded, and the first, rather inconclusive campaigns of the first Civil War had been fought. London, both the seat of Parliament and the stronghold of its support as well as Milton's birthplace and home, had for a while been under serious threat of royalist capture. But within the capital, a Puritan revolution continued apace. The Long Parliament convoked a standing conference of the principal theologians of the day, the Westminster Assembly of Divines, which met for the first time on 1 July 1643, charged with the thorough review of the doctrines and discipline of the Church of England, that secondary reformation that Milton had advocated in his antiprelatical pamphlets.

Milton's life records for the period of his silence are relatively thin. He did not seem to have taken up arms in the defense of the causes he had so vehemently defended with his pen. (Curiously, though, his brother, the lawyer Christopher, is listed on the muster roll of the royalist forces defending Reading, where he lived.[2] Christopher remained on good terms with John and lived to prosper, after a fashion, at the Restoration; as such, Christopher offers a timely reminder against any simple account of the social origins of the midcentury conflict.) We do know, however, that during this period, Milton married.

He thus rebuffed the Modest Confuter, who had charged him with ambitions of marrying a rich widow: "I care not if I tell him [the Confuter] thus much profestly, though it be to the losing of my *rich hopes,* as he calls them, that I think with them who both in prudence and elegance of spirit would choose a virgin of mean fortunes honestly bred, before the wealthiest widow" (*Apology, CPW,* I, 929). Of course, commentators have made much of this. Does it mean that Milton had, in general terms, resolved to marry and had determined the broad specifications of the ideal bride? Is it a sort of lonely hearts advertisement? Or does it show that he was thinking of one particular poor virgin? I hardly think it matters, nor may the issue now be resolved. But it does indicate very clearly that, in terms of how he conceptualizes or represents marriage, Milton is among the progressive element in his society, who looked beyond the marriage contract as a potentially profitable undertaking toward a more romantic and affectionate view.

Lawrence Stone has vividly charted the changes in the nature of marriage contracts in the early modern period. Among the most significant forces for change were radical Protestants who saw, in the developing nuclear family, a structure supportive of a worldview that put loyalty to personal belief above loyalty to kin and that conceived of salvation in terms of individual choice. Stone summarizes the revolution in sexual politics achieved in the seventeenth century:

> By 1700 there was clearly emerging among the bourgeois and landed gentry a new family type, . . . whose particular manifestations were as follows. The strength of the kin ties had declined and those that survived were increasingly limited to close relatives. Mate selection was determined more by free choice than by parental decision and was based as much on expectations of lasting mutual affection as on calculations of an increase in money, status or power. Except in the highest aristocratic circles, the financial considerations of the dowry and the jointure became less decisive elements in marriage negotiations than the prospect of future personal happiness based on settled and well-founded affection; as a result there were fewer marriages to heiresses, fewer marriages within the ramifications of the kin, and fewer marriages of young men to significantly older women.[3]

Stone, who alludes frequently to Milton as exemplar of this new agenda in interpersonal relationships, could be describing the pattern of Milton's first marriage.

For indeed Milton's first wife was both young (and in all likelihood virginal) and financially a poor catch.[4] She was Mary Powell, the eldest daughter of a gentry family from north Oxfordshire. Her father had borrowed money from Milton's father (and from many other moneylenders)—Milton's father had grown up a mile away from the Powell family home—and Milton knew the family from collecting the annual interest payment, which he did in the summer of 1642 when he met Mary Powell (possibly for the first time) and, after a short courtship, married her. Richard Powell's equity was in land, and it was heavily mortgaged through arrangements like the one he had entered into with the Milton family. Marriage settlements among the propertied classes in the early modern period characteristically included a dowry, usually property or a sum of money, paid by the bride's father to his son-in-law to compensate for the expense of keeping his daughter. The settlement Milton entered into initially may have seemed to be a good one, although he would almost certainly have known that Powell was getting into deep water with a whole array of moneylenders. In any event, the thousand pounds he was promised remained unpaid at his death in 1674.

But Milton, now 33, did get as his "virgin of mean fortunes," a woman of 17. She may well have been the first woman he had slept with. His earliest biographers concur that the relationship was initially not without its disappointments, and a short while later she returned to her family, with whom she resided for the next three years. It is altogether likely that the civil war was a factor—Oxford was the royalists' provisional capital, and Milton lived in the parliamentarian bastion of London. Quite possibly, the Powell family came to recognize difficulty in a marriage alliance with a Puritan activist, for they were committed royalists. We cannot now reconstruct what was going on inside their marriage, although it has been the subject of biographical speculation from the 1670s to the present day. However, we can reasonably suppose that personal events caused Milton's radical, questing mind to focus on an issue that did not much exercise his contemporaries: the issue of divorce reform.

Did Milton campaign for divorce reform in order that he might use new measures to divorce his wife? I doubt that the issues seemed so simple to him. There were surer ways to personal happiness that a little ethical casuistry could certainly have secured. But the campaign that he initiated in the summer of 1643 is wholly consonant with an elevated and progressive notion of the rewards of marriage and a sense that, if its better ends are frustrated by incompatibilities of an emotional or ideological or intellectual kind, then a remedy should be found in reform of the law. Milton carries through to a logical (but contemporaneously unacceptable) conclusion the elevation of the marriage bond that Stone identifies as central to a Puritan perspective on human relationships.

As the law stood in Milton's day, a divorce could be secured on the grounds of adultery, sexual incapacity, physical cruelty, or desertion. A divorce would not usually permit the remarriage of either party. Divorce was based on the fault of one of the partners. The fact that the marriage perhaps produced mutual unhappiness was of no significance in law. What usually mattered in divorce cases was essentially of a sexual nature. Could the couple copulate? Was a partner sexually faithful to the other? Milton of course understands that marriages are usually sexual relationships and that sexuality is an important component in marriage. Thus he notes that the dissatisfied husband, unable to divorce and remarry, is likely to "piece up his lost contentment by visiting the Stews, or stepping to his neighbours bed, which is the common shift in this mis-fortune" (*CPW,* II, 247). Milton has much to say about intellectual compatability between the sexes, but he knows that casual adultery and consorting with prostitutes have their origins elsewhere than in a love of good conversation.

The Doctrine and Discipline of Divorce

Recent critics, alert and sensitive to the nuances of gender politics, have remarked on the masculinism of Milton's tract. For a writer who supposedly longs for intellectual companionship from a woman and who advocates no-fault divorce, he nevertheless suggests a sustained image of the clever but naive husband forever yoked to someone who is dead from the neck up. Thus Mary Nyquist, with justification, complains,

> Yet much as the dominant discourse of the academy might like to celebrate this praiseworthy attention to mutuality, there are very few passages of any length in the divorce tracts that can be dressed up for the occasion. For over and over again, this laudable mutuality loses its balance, teetering precariously on the brink of pure abstraction. And the reason it does so is that it stands of the ground . . . of a lonely Adam who is not in any sense either ungendered or generic.[5]

Indeed so; the liberal academic tradition, with its received commitment to mutual respect between the sexes as the basis for heterosexual relationships, works to celebrate Milton's tract, but the tract itself, although it too celebrates mutuality in theory, is shot through with masculinist values.

Milton argues explicitly that woman is made for man; that a man has the responsibility to control and govern his wife; and that the great disparities in the status of the sexes justify his divorce reforms:

> For ev'n the freedom and eminence of mans creation gives him to be a Law in this matter to himself, beeing the head of the other sex which was made for him: whom therfore though he ought not to injure, yet neither should he be forc't to retain in society to his own overthrow, nor to hear any judge therin above himself. (*CPW*, II, 347)

He could scarcely speak plainer. This is no matter for the law to interfere in; if a man finds his wife to exhibit an "unpleasingnes" (*CPW*, II, 347), then she is sufficiently under his control, sufficiently (in a sense) in his possession, for him to decide to put her away without proving anything in court. It is a bit like owning a dog one cannot get along with; one can't be cruel to it, but it's nobody's business but the owner's if he decides to get rid of it.

These may well be Milton's real sentiments, but we shall never know, for this, like all his tracts, is an argument addressed to a target readership. The identity of that target readership is indicated clearly enough in the full title of the work: *The Doctrine and Discipline of Divorce: Restor'd to the Good of Both Sexes, From the bondage of Canon Law, and other mistakes, to Christian freedom, guided by the Rule of Charity. Wherein also many places of Scripture, have recover'd their long-lost meaning: Seasonable to be now thought on in the Reformation intended.* That intended Reformation is surely the work of the Westminster Assembly of Divines, set up by the Long Parliament, and the point is made explicit in the second edition of the pamphlet, issued in 1644, which has on its title page "To the Parlament of *England* with the Assembly," and which opens with a letter to the Parliament and the Assembly.

Milton correctly identified where the power to change the divorce law resided in the mid-1640s. If the Assembly had agreed with Milton, then Parliament would almost certainly have passed the appropriate legislation. His most important potential readers were austere Puritan divines and their political backers. Such men would certainly not have accepted the equality of women in any sphere of public or private life.

Moreover, they characteristically viewed human sexuality from an ascetic perspective. Draconian legislation was often considered, and at the end of the decade, an act was passed that actually provided for the death penalty for adultery.[6] In a late tract of the divorce series, Milton does let slip the view that, as Stephen Fallon glosses it, "a proper union of minds can lead to a better sex life."[7] But in *The Doctrine and Discipline,* Milton is much more guarded. He, too, gleefully anticipates draconian antifornication laws as the concomitant of his proposed changes in divorce: "then fornication shall be austerely censur'd, adultery punisht" (*CPW,* II, 279). Characteristically, sex is rather degraded into a messy necessity; it is "the quintessence of an excrement" (*CPW,* II, 248); the "work of male and female" (*CPW,* II, 240).

But not only does he attempt to trigger the repressive impulses of his target readers, he also makes a point pivotal to his argument. Hitherto, legislation had permitted divorce for carnal reasons such as sex outside marriage or sexual incapacity; but as the matters of the mind transcend matters of the flesh, so too a divorce law that takes notice of these lower matters should certainly be replaced by a divorce law that also takes notice of the higher matters.

For a modern reader, the most striking aspect of the text is probably the vividness with which he represents the horrors of a joyless marriage. Thus he ponders the spiritual status of the children of such a relationship, "the offspring of a[n] . . . ill-twisted wedlock, begott'n only out of a bestiall necessitie without any true love or contentment, or joy to their parents" (*CPW,* II, 259–60). Sex within such a marriage is "to grind in the mill of an undelighted and servil copulation" (*CPW,* II, 258—this passage was added to the second edition). Where there is no marriage of minds,

> instead of beeing one flesh, they will be rather two carkasses chain'd unnaturally together; or as it may happ'n, a living soule bound to a dead corpse, a punishment too like that inflicted by the tyrant *Mezentius.*[8]
> (*CPW,* II, 326–27)

Milton's argument, too, that sexual relationships should be more than merely sexual speaks to a modern reader the language of human affection, and indeed his position, favoring no-fault divorce by consent, has been English law since 1971. But for his contemporaries, his case stands or falls on the soundness of his theology.

For this is Milton's first theological treatise, his first attempt to build an argument on an original interpretation of the Bible. Here the problem is to reconcile texts that permit divorce with texts that forbid it. He founds his central proposition on Hebrew law:

> Deut. 24.1. *When a man hath tak'n a wife and married her, and it come to passe that she find no favour in his eyes, because he hath found some uncleanesse in her, let him write her a bill of divorcement, and give it in her hand, and send her out of his house, &c.* (quoted in *CPW,* II, 242).

The text itself is not unproblematic; inevitably a question arises about whether the kinds of intellectual and spiritual incompatabilities that interest Milton are covered by the term "some uncleanesse."

But the graver problem is that the New Testament is deemed to supersede the commandments of the Old where they differ, and what Christ has to say about divorce is altogether less permissive:

Matt. 5:31: It hath been said, Whosover shall put away his wife, let him give her a writing of divorcement;

32: But I say unto you, That whosoever shall put away his wife, saving for the cause of fornication, causeth her to commit adultery: and whosoever shall marry her that is divorced committeth adultery.

Matt. 19:3: The Pharisees also came unto him, tempting him, and saying unto him, Is it lawful for a man to put away his wife for every cause?

4: And he answered and said unto them, Have ye not read, that he which made them at the beginning made them male and female,

5: And said, For this cause shall a man leave father and mother, and shall cleave to his wife: and they twain shall be one flesh?

6: Wherefore they are no more twain, but one flesh.What therefore God hath joined together, let not man put asunder.

7: They say unto him, Why did Moses then command to give a writing of divorcement, and to put her away?

8: He saith unto them, Moses because of the hardness of your hearts suffered you to put away your wives: but from the beginning it was not so.

9: And I say unto you, Whosoever shall put away his wife, except it be for fornication, and shall marry another, committeth adultery: and whoso marrieth her which is put away doth commit adultery.

Milton has problems, and he can negotiate them only by convincing his readers that Christ's words are often not to be interpreted literally and that the seeming harshness of these passages runs counter to the larger Christian message of charity, in terms of which they must be reinterpreted. Although Milton had been plain enough in the antiprelatical campaign that the Bible gave guidance of sufficient clarity to resolve questions of church government, he now faced an altogether trickier task in reconciling different parts of the Bible. To interpret Christ properly, in Milton's view, it is necessary to contextualize his comments, which were part of a rebuke to Pharisees who were tempting him:

> The occasion which induc't our Saviour to speak of divorce, was either to convince the extravagance of the Pharises in that point, or to give a sharp and vehement answer to a tempting question. And in such cases that we are not to repose all upon the literall terms of so many words, many instances will teach us: Wherin we may plainly discover how Christ meant not to be tak'n word for word, but like a wise Physician, administring one excesse against another to reduce us to a perfect mean: Where the Pharises were strict, there Christ seems remisse; where they were too remisse, he saw it needfull to seem most severe. (*CPW,* II, 282–83)

Thus, Milton's interpretative strategy invokes some of the variables a modern critic should bring to a consideration of Civil War polemic, especially a sense of the occasion of the comments and of the intended audience. It is a bold critical maneuver, and on its own terms probably unconvincing. Christ's message seems clear enough, however unwelcome it may be to those unhappily married in an age of faith.

Milton has another cluster of problems to negotiate relating to the original institution of marriage. Genesis implies the permanence in that striking phrase "they shall be one flesh" (2:24). Milton has to argue that that term applies to a sound marriage that realizes the explicit objectives of marriage, namely that God made a "help meet" for Adam to assuage his loneliness (2:18). Milton thus makes the larger statement dependent on the assertion of the purpose of the institution, and again he foregrounds not the reproductive directives of Genesis 1:28 ("be fruitful, and multiply") but the companionship implicit in the recognition of Adam's loneliness.

Milton may quite reasonably have thought that, if he had carried the theological argument, he would have carried the Assembly with him and thereafter the Long Parliament. For all its radicalism, *The Doctrine and Discipline of Divorce* is a tract he advances as a continuation of his earlier writing and as an initiative in broad accord with the developing radicalism of Parliament. But whatever his expectations, his experience in the months following its publication demonstrated crushingly his powerlessness to change government policy. Far from influencing those that mattered, he himself was taken up as an example, a case study, in why the state should suppress such heterodoxy.

The reasons can be identified with some facility. Toward the close of the antiprelatical campaign, Milton had become increasingly drawn to the question of uniformity within a newly reformed state church and of the toleration of heterodox opinion. Thus he had been drawn to pondering the role of the sects in the immediate circumstances.[9] His concerns largely reflect the anxieties of other Puritans. Indeed, the newly convoked Westminster Assembly of Divines had been divided over the issues, and a small but able Independent minority had formed, who advocated congregational independency and a considerable degree of toleration.[10] Presbyterians and their allies, in the Assembly, in Parliament, and in the larger London community, were numerically strong and well organized, and from 1643 until late in the decade, they mounted a sustained and coordinated campaign.

Milton's antiprelatical tracts had achieved some attention; there are contemporary references to them extant, and *Animadversions* had obviously irked the group around Joseph Hall sufficiently to provoke the response of the *Modest Confutation*. But *The Doctrine and Discipline of Divorce* rapidly became notorious. Habitually it was linked with two other contemporaneously sensational works, *Mans Mortallitie* (Amsterdam, 1643; London, 1644) and *The Bloudy Tenent of Persecution for Cause of Conscience* (London, 1644). This, in radical terms, is rather high-profile company. The former, whose anonymous author, R. O., is almost certainly Richard Overton, the future Leveler leader, was first published abroad—a good indicator of its potential for attracting trouble. The latter was the work of Roger Williams, a founder of the radical Puritan community of Rhode Island, who had lately returned to represent the new colony's interests to the Long Parliament. *Mans Mortallitie* disputes the orthodox view that each soul receives a separate judgment on death and is assigned to its destination while the body awaits resurrection at the Second Coming. It is a mortalist work that, with great élan, argues instead that soul and body sleep in the grave until their eventual resurrection together. This doctrine was contemporaneously extremely heretical (although it was entertained by figures as unradical as Thomas

Browne and Thomas Hobbes). Williams's tract, often cited as an analogue to Milton's slightly later *Areopagitica,* is a tolerationist work, although it is a tolerationism couched in millenarian terms—because the Second Coming is imminent and final judgment is at hand, all positions may as well be tolerated. Williams's modern biographer has termed it, perhaps a little excessively, "one of the greatest—if also one of the most gnarled and incoherent—utterances in the language."[11] Together the three authors exemplify three principal aspects of religious radicalism—R. O. represents zany ideas from Continental sources (evidenced by the Dutch imprint); Williams shows the dangers of letting go the reins of doctrinal constraint; and Milton can be presented as a sexual libertine, destroying the permanency of the marriage bond that constitutes the foundation of the social fabric and with it of the preservation and legitimate transfer of property.

Although Milton's tract did not impact seriously on the deliberations of the Assembly or of the Long Parliament, it certainly attracted a readership. He reissued it in a second edition, somewhat expanded as we shall see, in February 1644. By July 1645 he tells us that it was virtually sold out—the tract has been "twice printed, twice bought up" (*CPW,* II, 436)—and it was reprinted twice more in 1645. No early work by him had seen even a second edition. Second and subsequent print runs for works that proved to be strong selling were probably longer than the initial print run, so we may reasonably speculate that the book was in circulation in the low thousands by 1645, an early but convincing demonstration that nothing boosts sales better than attempts at suppression.

The Doctrine and Discipline, second edition, and *The Judgment of Martin Bucer*

By the end of 1643, Milton had in effect pitched tent in the camp of the Independent opponents of Presbyterianism, and this affiliation remains ideologically his lasting commitment. He was further radicalized along with that faction, but the allies of 1643 were his allies in 1649 and 1660. He could scarcely have imagined what a process of revolutionary change he was enlisting in.

More astute Independents than Milton recognized the political realities of their position and sought out other routes. As Ernest Sirluck notes, Milton's later appeals to the Assembly take place after others of his radical kidney had abandoned hope of progress through that agency.[12] He remains almost obsessed with addressing Parliament, although a shrewder analysis would have indicated its futility. Milton retained for a surprising while a naive belief in the capacity of reason and eloquence to influence the course of political history.

His first move after the initial publication of *The Doctrine and Discipline* was to revise it for reissue. If we focus our analysis on the style of the two editions, and in particular on the similes and metaphors woven into the fabric of his prose, important distinctions emerge. Milton's antiprelatical tracts are stylistically very vivid, and the points he makes often find most telling expression as an extended metaphor or simile, in passages such as the one that extended comparison of prelacy to a "Wen" or wart, "a heape of hard, and loathsome uncleannes . . . a foul disfigurment and burden" (*CPW*, I, 583–84, discussed in chapter 3). That idiom is wholly characteristic of all the antiprelatical tracts. But in the first edition of *The Doctrine and Discipline,* he produces for the first time another prose voice, much less vivid and much more engaged in the sober transmission of argument. Certainly, as we saw earlier, the tract contains some images of enormous imaginative power, but they are much less frequent. However, the material he added to the second edition is so heavy with imagery that its plain sense is sometimes quite hard to follow. In the new epistle with which he opens the tract, almost every sentence has an image, and the imagery is perplexingly repetitive as the same point of comparison is reworked and reapplied. In the original, Truth is conceptualized as a woman in labor, whose "womb" is not "to be clos'd up" (*CPW*, II, 224); but on the same page of the original edition, Truth is now the issue of that labor, its object, not its subject:

> For Truth is as impossible to be soil'd by any outward touch, as the Sun beam. Though this ill hap wait on her nativity, that shee never comes into the world, but like a Bastard, to the ignominy of him that brought her forth: till Time the Midwife rather then the mother of Truth, have washt and salted the Infant, declar'd her legitimat, and Churcht the father of his young *Minerva,* from the needlesse causes of his purgation. (*CPW*, II, 225)

Readers may admit an initial surprise that the mother of truth is in this case a "he"; but Milton, in attempting to give his tract the stylistic impact of his antiprelatical pamphlets, gets himself increasing tangled. Truth has been a mother; next she's a sunbeam; next he, Milton, is a father but a father that, in a perverse parthenogenesis, gives birth to a child of his own conceiving. The image then mutates into a literary grotesque that, as the editor of the Yale edition notes, integrates allusion to classical myth with the details of the Anglican service of churching women after childbirth.[13]

So Milton, as if wobbling in his original confidence that a plain argument unflamboyantly advanced will persuade fellow Puritans, trowels the imagery on, bringing this tract, as revised, into line with his mode of exposition in his earlier works. He also points up more sharply his primary readership, buttonholing them in that wholly new epistle, which is addressed "To the Parliament of England, with the Assembly" (*CPW,* II, 222–33). That new epistle is designed to stimulate appropriate impulses in their collective consciousness, and in panegyric mode it eloquently suggests both that the time is uniquely right for reformation and that they are uniquely equipped to effect it. It ends with a courteous (almost courtly) coda of poise and eloquence:

> [*The Doctrine and Discipline*] might perhaps more fitly have bin writt'n in another tongue; and I had don so, but that the esteem I have of my Countries judgement, and the love I beare to my native language to serv it first with what I endeavour, made me speak it thus, ere I assay the verdit of outlandish readers. And perhaps also heer I might have ended nameles [i.e., anonymous], but that the addresse of these lines chiefly to the Parliament of *England* might have seem'd ingratefull not to acknowledge by whose Religious care, unwearied watchfulnes, couragious and heroick resolutions, I enjoy the peace and studious leisure to remain,
>   *The Honourer and Attendant of their Noble worth and vertues,*
>   John Milton.

The Reason of Church-Government had carried Milton's name (though *An Apology,* curiously for a personal defense, had not). Milton had issued the first edition of *The Doctrine and Discipline* anonymously, perhaps in that gesture trusting to the argument to speak for itself. When he reissues it, the title page carries his initials and the epistle his full name. Plainly this is a work he stands by and invites his adversaries to a proper debate.

There are other significant changes to the title page. The first edition carried the initials of the printers; the second edition does not—we shall return to this point when we consider *Areopagitica.* The first edition carried one epigraph, from Matthew 13:52, "*Every Scribe instructed to the Kingdome of Heav'n, is like the Maister of a house which bringeth out of his treasurie things old and new.*" In the second edition, he adds from Proverbs 18:13, "*He that answereth a matter before he heareth it, it is folly and shame unto him."* Milton alludes to the attack on his book and to the absence of real intellectual engagement with it. The epigraph indicates clearly that the author of *Animadversions* and *An Apology* is on the counterattack.

The second edition appeared in February 1644. In July 1644 Milton published his first extended work of translation—a work once more addressed on its title page "To the Parlament of England"—*The Iudgement of Martin Bucer, concerning Divorce, Writt'n to* Edward *the sixt, in his second Book of the Kingdom of Christ. And now English. Wherin a late Book restoring the* Doctrine and Discipline of Divorce, *is heer confirm'd and justify'd by the authoritie of Martin Bucer.* Once more the epigraph, here from John 3:10, signals the aggressive intent: "Art thou a teacher of Israel, and know'st not these things?"

Martin Bucer (1491–1551) could scarcely have been a better figure for Milton's purpose. He was a Dominican friar who became an early and significant supporter of Luther, to whom he remained theologically close. A Protestant leader in Strasbourg, he was driven from the city by the Catholic Holy Roman Emperor, Charles V, and fled for asylum to the England of Edward VI, where he was received with honor. He was appointed to a chair in Cambridge although he died shortly afterward, but after the accession of the Catholic Mary I, his body was exhumed and burned. The familiar line against Independents and sectaries is that they represent a continuity with groups like the Münsterian Anabaptists, a kind of third force as separate from the Protestantism of Luther or Calvin as that was from Roman Catholicism. Indeed, Luther had sanctioned the sack of Münster and the suppression of its Anabaptist leaders. But if Milton can demonstrate that Bucer agrees with Milton and that Bucer was close to and respected by Protestants of Luther's age, then that stratagem is thwarted.

Milton accomplishes this objective with great élan. The book is prefaced with "Testimonies of the high approbation Which learned men have given of *Martin Bucer*" (*CPW,* II, 422–29), most of which come from the edition of Bucer he was using, although he adds material from Foxe's *Acts and Monuments* and from standard histories and biographies of reformed divines.[14] What emerges is not only Bucer's Protestant respectability but also his status as Protestant martyr, hounded from his homeland, sheltered by Edward VI, and posthumously abused by Catholics. Milton adds, too, the analogy between his own view of divorce and that of Paulus Fagius, another reformed divine with a curriculum vitae very similar to Bucer's. The subtext is clear: if Milton is to continue to be hounded by Presbyterians and the like, then they are behaving like the

Catholics and he resembles the authentic Protestant martyr. As he puts it
in the epistle to Parliament, which carries his name:

> *Not that I have now more confidence* [in the arguments advanced in his first
> divorce tract] *by the addition of these great Authors to my party; for what I
> wrote was not my opinion, but my knowledge; evn then when I could trace no foot-
> step in the way I went: nor that I think to win upon your apprehensions with
> numbers and with names, rather then with reasons, yet certainly the worst of my
> detracters will not except against so good a baile of my integritie and judgement,
> as now appeares for me. They must els put in the fame of* Bucer *and* Fagius, *as
> my accomplices and confederats into the same endightment; they must dig up the
> good name of these prime worthies (if thir names could be ever buried), they must
> dig them up and brand them as the Papists did thir bodies; and those thir pure
> unblamable spirits, which live not only in heaven, but in thir writings, they must
> attaint with new attaintures which no Protestant ever before aspers't them with.*
> (*CPW,* II, 439 – 40)

Milton does not say that his arguments are sounder because Bucer and
his associate Fagius shared them. But he does say that his arguments
deserve respect from Puritan divines because, far from characterizing the
ideology of some intolerable fanatic, they are shared by men close to
Luther who were civilly entertained in the England of Edward VI, whose
reign in Puritan belief constituted a sort of golden age precursory to the
secondary reformation of the 1640s. Morover, as the epigraph asserts,
Presbyterians who traduce him do so out of ignorance of the historical
bona fides of his arguments.

Milton translates from the Latin of Bucer's *De Regno Christi* [*On the
Kingdom of Christ*], first published in 1551, arguments for divorce reform
that surprisingly approximate his own. No doubt as he says, he was
unaware of Bucer's views when he formed his, but the congruities must
have pleased him greatly, as in:

> Our Saviour came to preach repentance, and remission; seeing ther-
> fore those who put away thir wives without any just cause, were not
> toucht with conscience of the sin, through misunderstanding of the law,
> he recall'd them to a right interpretation, and taught that the woman in
> the beginning was so joyn'd to the man, that there should be a perpet-
> ual union both in body and spirit: where this is not, the matrimony is
> already broke, before there be yet any divorce made or second mariage.
> (*CPW,* II, 456)

Alhough the style of the translation is relatively anonymous, following as it must the Latin of Bucer, the tract nevertheless develops a restrained eloquence and works with a polemical power to destabilize Milton's attackers, making them seem the enemies, not the heirs, to the great tradition of Protestant reform and the real threat to the vital work in progress. As Milton summarizes it in his postscript,

> I bid this Kingdom beware: and doubt not but God who hath dignify'd this Parlament already to so many glorious degrees, will also give them (which is a singular blessing) to inform themselvs rightly in the midst of an unprincipl'd age; and to prevent this working mystery of ignorance and ecclesiastical thraldom, which under new shapes and disguises begins afresh to grow upon us. (*CPW*, II, 479)

Milton had not finished with his detractors. Some seven months after *Bucer*, he published the curiously complementary tracts *Tetrachordon* and *Colasterion*, probably on the same day in early March 1645 and from the same print shop.[15]

Tetrachordon and *Colasterion*

Tetrachordon, written in that less figurative style Milton had experimented with in the earliest edition of *The Doctrine and Discipline,* is, as the title page explains, a series of "Expositions Upon The foure chief places in Scripture, which treat of Mariage, or nullities in Mariage." Generically, it is an exegetical treatise; that is, it is a work of theology concerned with explaining or interpreting the scriptures. Its title is, of course, rather puzzling, and in a poem probably written shortly after its publication, Milton remarks on its role in the reception the book received:

> A book was writ of late called *Tetrachordon*;
>   And woven close, both matter, form and style;
>   The subject new: it walked the town awhile,
>   Numbering good intellects; now seldom pored on.
> Cries the stall-reader, Bless us! what a word on
>   A title-page is this! And some in file
>   Stand spelling false, while one might walk to Mile-
>   End Green.[16]

Milton had fallen into a habit of having rather obscure titles for his pamphlets—*Areopagitica,* to which we shall shortly turn, and now these two. This poem seems to indicate that Milton recognized that his title may have put off simple readers.

Milton has borrowed the word itself directly from classical Greek, in which it was the name of a four-stringed musical instrument. A word derived from it, "tetrachord," had some limited currency in contemporary English, meaning either the same classical instrument or a scale-series of four notes or the interval between the first and last notes of such a series.[17] But it must have been a rare word or the readers browsing the bookstalls would not have taken exception to it.

Of course, Milton uses the word metaphorically; this is a tract that plays in harmony the four principal texts that relate to divorce, namely Genesis 1:27–28, Deuteronomy 24:1, Matthew 5:31–32, and I Corinthians 7. It is a long book, some 97 pages in the original, longer than the second edition of *The Doctrine and Discipline* and four times the length of *Bucer*. His method is a patient teasing out of the texts, glossing and supplementing them by cross-reference to other biblical material, and evidently he feels no constraints of space. Thus he argues that the words in Deuteronomy that permit a man to divorce his wife if the man finds "some uncleanesse" in her is of wider implication than the discovery of some sexual impurity. Milton takes some 11 pages in the original to work through the arguments, which he introduces as an ordered sequence: "For first . . . Secondly . . . Twelfthly . . . These reasons, and many more that might bee alleg'd, afford us plainly to perceav" (*CPW,* II, 621–32). His prose is cool, his energy focused on the methodical substantiation of an often technical argument, although there are occasionally more flamboyant (and memorable) passages, as when, glossing the Genesis injunction that man and wife shall be "one flesh," he reminds us,

> nature teaches us to divide any limb from the body to the saving of his fellows, though it be the maiming and deformity of the whole; how much more is it her doctrin to sever by incision, not a true limb so much, though that be lawfull, but an adherent, a sore, the gangrene of a limb, to the recovery of a whole man. (*CPW,* II, 602)

But it is at his most vivid that Milton, the advocate of divorce, can seem most disturbing and disturbed. His larger argument, that marriage finds its proper godly fulfillment not only in sexual relations but also in emotional, ideological, and intellectual compatibility, is decent and humane. But his vehemence about the horrors of a failed marriage seems ill-matched to his elevated and idealized thesis and finds expression in images of decaying corpses shackled to living people and rotting flesh to be gouged out in desperate, primitive surgery. These images are of close physical proximity of a disgusting kind and point to the poisoned and immature sensibility of a would-be Cathar horrified by the sexual congress he has effected, reifying and rejecting the loved one he has penetrated as something foully sullying.[18] The gender politics are disturbing too. Again, at a certain level of abstraction, Milton appears to value women more highly than his male contemporaries did, requiring from the marriage bond much more than a ready sexual partner, a dowry, and a mechanism for the survival of the family line. But in these grotesque images the gendering is unmistakable: Adam and the sons of Adam are the body to be saved, and women are the gangrenous infection upon which the surgeon's knife must fall.

Colasterion complements *Tetrachordon*. Like that tract, *Colasterion* has an obscure name of classical Greek origin; it is simply a transcription of a word meaning a place or instrument of punishment. Its editor suggests that in choosing this word for his title, Milton may have had in mind a turn of phrase from Lucian's satiric dialogue *Menippus,* set in the classical Underworld: "Leaving then the place of judgment, we came to the place of punishment."[19] The implication of this choice would be that Milton in *Tetrachordon* effected judgment in the issues of divorce; in *Colasterion* he merely beats the condemned.

The condemned in question is primarily the anonymous author of *An Answer to a Book, Intituled, The Doctrine and Discipline of Divorce, or, A Plea for Ladies and Gentlewomen, and all other Maried Women against Divorce,* published late in 1644, although in *Colasterion*, Milton also swipes at others who had more briefly criticized his divorce tracts. The anonymous answerer produced the only tract-length response to Milton's radical thesis; all the attempts to provoke those who resisted his proposed reforms ended in merely this pamphlet. His adversary evidently had thought fit to answer only the first edition, ignoring the considered additions Milton had made to it. Moreover, in an intellectual landscape dominated by the Westminster Assembly of Divines, which included some of the best Puritan theologians in midcentury England, Milton's work is matched rather by a virtually unknown figure with almost no academic credentials. Milton has discovered, or purports to have discovered, that his enemy, perhaps aided by others, was a serving man who had improved his condition by becoming a lawyer. *Colasterion* is thus offered as a sort of joke among gentlemen at the expense of a member of the lower classes who has raised himself above his station:

the cheif [of his respondents] . . . was intimated to mee, and since ratifi'd
to bee no other, if any can hold laughter, and I am sure none will guess
him lower, then an actual Serving-man. This creature, for the Story must
on, (and what though hee bee the lowest person of an interlude, hee may
deserv a canvasing,) transplanted himself, and to the improvment of his
wages, and your better notice of his capacity, turn'd Solliciter. (*CPW*, II,
726–27)

This short tract, some 27 pages in the original, sustains this tone of
supercilious sneering and studied class prejudice. The title is part of that
joke, for Milton claims to know, from errors in his adversary's refutation,
that he does not know Greek, "and is not able to spell it" (*CPW*, II, 724).
But why would he know it? He is a working man. Milton proceeds
pretty much as he had against Hall in *Animadversions,* adapting academic disputation into a polemic that quotes or paraphrases the enemy
and then offers a comment. But here, when he has after a fashion let the
enemy speak, he comes in with a tart reminder of his enemy's class
background:

> But hee goes on to untruss my Arguments, imagining them his Mais-
> ters points [that is, he unties Milton's arguments as if he were untying
> the laces which hold the parts of his master's clothes together]. (*CPW*, II,
> 743)
> Finally, hee windes up his Text with much doubt and trepidation; for
> it may bee his trenchers were not scrap't. . . .
> After waiting and voiding, hee thinks to void my second Argument
> [that is, he seems anxious, as if he remembers he hasn't done the dishes;
> and then he attempts to clear away Milton's argument, much as once he
> cleared tables]. (*CPW*, II, 746)

Perhaps the most savage blow comes when Milton's adversary is arguing
that it is all very well to talk about marriage in terms of intellectual
companionship but sex produces offspring, and sometimes the divorced
woman may be carrying a child when her dissatisfied partner dismisses
her: it "must needs bee good news for Chamber-maids, to hear a Serving-man grown so provident for great bellies" (*CPW*, II, 734), a simple
insult both to his enemy and to the morality of the working class—what
a splendid thing that a servant, usually keen on seducing chambermaids
and so indifferent as to whether he gets them pregnant, should now find
himself thinking about these things.

There is another angle of attack, a narrow, focused name-calling. His
enemy had discussed marriage and the grounds for divorce primarily in

those sexual terms that Milton had sought to redefine, or better still, to set aside in favor of his more humane arguments. So Milton brands this man as a creature that cannot raise his thoughts from carnality. Scarcely a man, he is "a Boar in a Vinyard" chewing over his thesis; "this Barrow [castrated boar—a curious detail] grunt[s]" at a word Milton uses; he is a "snout" (all from *CPW*, II, 747); "I mean not to dispute Philosophy with this Pork, who never read any" (*CPW*, II, 737); "Came this doctrin out of som School, or som stie?" (*CPW*, II, 739).

But the pig imagery is yet another manifestation of the class prejudice, a strategy of exclusion from the discourse of gentlemen: "This is not for an unbutton'd fellow to discuss in the Garret, at his tressle" (*CPW*, II, 746). Persistently Milton calls on his reader over the head of his adversary, and he calls on him as his equal, urging that, metaphorically, they treat the uppity servant with rough play, that they give him "a canvasing" (*CPW*, II, 726) or that they "blanket" him (*CPW*, II, 754), stripping him of his disguise of professional status and humiliating him like robust undergraduates tossing an offending college servant in a sheet.

In our seemingly more egalitarian age, in which class prejudice takes far subtler forms, Milton's admirers must wince at this. It is easy enough to see the game he is playing. The speculative theology of the kind Milton has drifted into was contemporaneously associated by its enemies with sectaries, and sectaries were always represented as lower-class tradesmen preachers in trades like felt making, sow spaying, and button making. Milton gets in among stereotypers, spoiling their game. The Presbyterians' champion is himself a serving man, albeit one that has improved himself a bit. Milton, a rich man's son who may well not have earned a penny in his life thus far, talks to other gentlemen, including gentlemen Presbyterians, who really should have known better than to hire a mere servant.

So Milton's motivation is clear enough. Nevertheless *Colasterion* remains the most sustained exposition of unacceptable social values in his whole oeuvre. He does include one undeveloped gesture of qualification when he remarks that working men, though their prose style may be "flat and rude," may occasionally produce something "grave and solid" (*CPW*, II, 725). The midcentury saw the production of some quite extraordinary prose by working men, in the Digger socialist manifestos of Gerrard Winstanley and a little later the undeferential narratives of John Bunyan. But for Milton the unpropertied had no stake in the political nation, no stake really in the higher discourses of politics and theology currently so fissuring and animating the intellectual life of England.

Explaining in *Tetrachordon* why Christ in Matthew 19 had spoken harshly to the Pharisees, he remarks, "We doe not say to a servant what we say to a sonne" (*CPW,* II, 643); Milton rather forgets the ancient notion of Christianity as a discourse that speaks to all people.

Areopagitica

In November 1644, about halfway between the publication of *Bucer* and *Tetrachordon,* Milton published *Areopagitica; A Speech of Mr. John Milton For the Liberty of Unlicenc'd Printing, To the Parlament of England.* It is by some margin his most famous prose work, frequently reprinted over the centuries, often translated, and often quoted and cited as an eloquent formulation of central tenets of liberal belief. Its origins, however, rest wholly in his campaign for divorce reform.

Areopagitica is a tolerationist pamphlet, analogous in some ways to Roger Williams's *Bloudy Tenent of Persecution,* which we considered earlier in the chapter. As such, it shares common ground with the Independent or Congregationalist arguments that the Protestant community in England should be a very broad church allowing a whole range of practices and beliefs within agreements about its distinctiveness from Catholicism. Milton speaks the language of that movement when he complains, "We [that is, English Protestants in general] stumble and are impatient at the least dividing of one visible congregation from another, though it be not in fundamentalls" (*CPW,* II, 564). It is not the "visible congregation" of a unified state church that matters; what matters, according to Milton, is a healthy and active dialogue within a broader Protestant community that allows dissent and admits that all the answers to the problems of Christian life are not yet known.

But *Areopagitica* is focused on a particular aspect of tolerationism (one that has rendered it so important to liberal sentiment): freedom of the press. Continuing debate is not possible without relatively unfettered access to the press, as both Milton and his enemies recognized. Two principal strategies for press control existed in the early modern period: either one could wait until a book was published, prosecute its author, printer, and bookseller, and call in the book and have it destroyed; or one could insist that no book be printed until its manuscript had first been examined by an appointed officer and passed as fit for publication. The latter, which is called licensing, was the favored mechanism in seventeenth-century England. It was the system perfected in the closing years of the personal rule of Charles I. The Star Chamber, a high court by which much of the social and political control of the country was effected, decreed in 1637 a series of measures that elaborated and confirmed earlier legislation. Books were to be examined by clergy appointed by the Bishop of London or the Archbishop of Canterbury; the system was to be policed by the Stationers Company, which was the guild or trade association for printers and booksellers:

> no person or persons whatsoever, shall at any time print or cause to be imprinted, any Booke or Pamphlet whatsoever, unlesse the same Booke or Pamphlet, and also all and every the Titles, Epistles, Prefaces, Proems, Preambles, Introductions, Tables, Dedications, and other matters and things whatsoever thereunto annexed, or therewith imprinted, shall be first lawfully licenced and authorized only by such person and persons as are hereafter expressed, and by no other, and shall be also first entred into the Registers Booke of the Company of Stationers; upon paine that every Printer offending therein, shall be for ever hereafter disabled to use or exercise the Art or Mysterie of Printing, and receive such further punishment, as by this Court or the high Commission Court respectively, as the severall causes shall require, shall be thought fitting.[20]

The law allowed the Star Chamber court to do pretty much as it liked with those convicted under it. It reflects that obsession with suppressing dissent that characterized 1637, the pivotal year in the fortunes of Charles I and his radical opponents. The force of that legislation effectively ended with the dissolution of the Star Chamber court, but in June 1643 Parliament passed the Licensing Order, which restated its principal measures with necessary changes in the process of enforcement and in the appointment of the licensers (Parliament would scarcely have asked Archbishop Laud to nominate the licensers):

> [no] Book, Pamphlet, paper, nor part of any such Book, Pamphlet, or paper, shall from henceforth be printed, bound, stitched or put to sale by any person or persons whatsoever, unlesse the same be first approved of and licensed under the hands of such person or persons as both, or either of the said Houses shall appoint for the licensing of the same, and entred in the Register Book of the Company of *Stationers,* according to Ancient custom, and the Printer therof to put his name thereto.[21]

The phrasing of the legislation and the invocation of "Ancient custom" indicate clearly enough the lineage of the measure.

Of course Parliament had broader concerns than suppressing unusual proposals for divorce reform, and indeed the law antedates the first edition of *The Doctrine and Discipline* by two months. Quite simply, those who were in control of the political institutions in London and Westminster were very alarmed by the massive increases in press activity since the calling of the Long Parliament. George Thomason, a London bookseller, began in 1640 to collect the output of the press into what became by the Restoration a library of some 15,000 individual titles, plus thousands of issues of periodicals. The early 1640s are particularly heavily represented within the collection.[22]

The first edition of *The Doctrine and Discipline* had carried the initials of its printers; the second and subsequent editions did not. *Bucer* was licensed and carried the printer's name. *Areopagitica,* like *Tetrachordon* and *Colasterion,* did not. An analysis of tracts published in middecade shows that the Licensing Order was most scrupulously followed by those authors who were ideologically aligned with the Presbyterians and others who had promoted the legislation; writers of a heterodox or radical aspect, those whom it was intended to suppress, for the most part ignored and defied it.[23] But Milton puts his own name or initials on these dissident publications, and *Areopagitica* carries his full name in large uppercase italics. He is not afraid of prosecution and is willing to defend himself in open court from any charge of heresy or blasphemy (which would have been a defense of sorts against the obvious violation of the Licensing Order). Indeed, in December 1644, on the advice of senior officers of the Stationers Company, the House of Lords instructed two justices to "examine" Milton about his recent publications. The record does not disclose the outcome of this order, but his earliest biographer concludes of the incident, "that house, whether approving the Doctrin, or not favoring his Accusers, soon dismiss'd him."[24]

The incident will probably remain enigmatic. *Areopagitica* has clear enough objectives, however: it seeks to persuade Parliament to replace licensing with postpublication responsibility before the law. It sets a narrow pale to the ideologies that may thus be tolerated:

> if all cannot be of one mind, as who looks they should be? this doubtles is more wholsome, more prudent, and more Christian that many be tolerated, rather then all compell'd. I mean not tolerated Popery, and open superstition, which as it extirpats all religions and civill supremacies, so it self should be extirpat, provided first that all charitable and compassionat means be us'd to win and regain the weak and the misled: that also which is impious or evil absolutely against faith or maners no law can possibly permit, that intends not to unlaw it self: but those neighboring differences, or rather indifferences, are what I speak of, whether in some point of doctrine or of discipline, which though they may be many,

> yet need not interrupt *the unity of Spirit,* if we could but find among us *the bond of peace.* (*CPW,* II, 565)

Milton agrees, then, that a line must be drawn to exclude the unacceptable from the press, but disagrees where the line should be drawn. It is not absolutely clear whether "Popery, and open superstition" simply means Catholicism and *its* superstitious practices or whether it means Catholicism and *other* superstitious practices (such as Laudian ceremonialism). Because Catholicism asserts the preeminence of the rule of the Pope over the civil government of nations, it is a threat to the autonomy of those nations. Because, through agencies of the Counter-Reformation such as the Inquisition, Catholicism suppresses Protestantism where it can and thus (in Milton's view) all godliness, it should itself be suppressed. In the same way, opinions that are "impious or evil," presumably ones condemned by a wide consensus of Protestant opinion, need not be tolerated. Earlier in the tract, Milton expressed the view that the primary organ of royalist propaganda, the newspaper *Mercurius Aulicus,* already subject to an ineffectual ban, should be suppressed (*CPW,* II, 528). As Milton puts it early in the tract, "I deny not, but that it is of greatest concernment . . . to have a vigilant eye how Bookes demeane themselves, as well as men; and thereafter to confine, imprison, and do sharpest justice on them as malefactors" (*CPW,* II, 492).

Milton has been accused of falling somewhat short of the liberal ideal. Such issues, though, are rarely simple. London was the capital of a state at war; it was unreasonable that the other side should be free to disseminate its version of events, and the suppression of *Mercurius Aulicus* was no more than the equivalent of radio jamming. Currently, legislation in the United Kingdom forbids the distribution of material intended to incite racial abuse; the line may be drawn differently, but it is still drawn. The history of the Weimar Republic shows all too vividly the fate of a liberal regime too tolerant of its enemies.

But the problem with *Areopagitica* is not that it limits toleration but that it bases some of its case on a cluster of arguments that point to complete toleration. Milton seeks to define behavior that is meritorious in God's sight in terms of resistance to temptation. If Christians are not exposed to arguments that tempt them into heretical belief or behavior, then they do not earn the reward belonging to those who are tested and who stand firm:

> He that can apprehend and consider vice with all her baits and seeming pleasures, and yet abstain, and yet distinguish, and yet prefer that which

is truly better, he is the true warfaring Christian. I cannot praise a fugitive and cloister'd vertue, unexercis'd & unbreath'd, that never sallies out and sees her adversary, but slinks out of the race, where that immortall garland is to be run for, not without dust and heat. Assuredly we bring not innocence into the world, we bring impurity much rather: that which purifies us is triall, and triall is by what is contrary. That vertue therefore which is but a youngling in the contemplation of evill, and knows not the utmost that vice promises to her followers, and rejects it, is but a blank vertue, not a pure; her whitenesse is but an excrementall whitenesse. (*CPW,* II, 514–16)

Fine words, but the contemplation of evil in its most extreme, for a seventeenth-century Protestant, most surely included contemplation of Catholicism, with its seductive theology of indulgence and saintly mediation and its promise of salvation standing open to all, its comforting rituals, and astonishingly beautiful art and architecture. "Popery" has to be tolerated to know "the utmost that vice promises to her followers." Again, godliness is something to be arrived at through the spiritual exercise of confronting its opposite, and the more powerful the opponent, the greater the spiritual advantage: why not then engagement with Catholicism?

Again, at his most eloquent, he asserts:

though all the windes of doctrin were let loose to play upon the earth, so Truth be in the field, we do injuriously by licencing and prohibiting to misdoubt her strength. Let her and Falshood grapple; who ever knew Truth put to the wors, in a free and open encounter. Her confuting is the best and surest suppressing. (*CPW,* II, 561)

"Free and open encounter" may suggest that, in circumstances where Truth is not freely disseminated, Falsehood should also be suppressed. But such circumstances need scarcely apply in Civil War London, for *Mercurius Aulicus* was matched by any number of pro-Parliament newsbooks and journals, and the mighty Westminster Assembly of Divines stood ready to respond to Catholic doctrine. So if Truth does indeed always beat Falsehood in a fair fight, why then should there be legislation to suppress Catholicism and royalist propaganda? "Confuting is the best . . . suppressing." Again, "To the pure all things are pure, not only meats and drinks, but all kinde of knowledge whether of good or evill; the knowledge cannot defile, nor consequently the books, if the will and conscience be not defil'd" (*CPW,* II, 512). Why not the knowledge, then, of subtle Catholic theology or the claims of the royalist propaganda machine?

We look for coherence and do not find it. Perhaps Milton, as Stanley Fish has argued, expresses an ultimate indifference to the issue of press freedom that is premised on a recognition that books are inherently no more a force for evil than they are for good, and that whatever godliness we may arrive at comes from the spirit within rather than from external human agency:

> In short, the argument against licensing, which has always been read as an argument *for* books, is really an argument that renders books beside the point; books are no more going to save you than they are going to corrupt you; by denying their potency in one direction, Milton necessarily denies their potency in the other and undercuts the extravagant claims he himself makes. . . . Whatever books are, they cannot be what he says they are in those ringing sentences, the preservers of truth, the life-blood of a master spirit, the image of God.[25]

These are shrewd comments, but they elide the distinction Milton habitually makes between his own writing and other people's. Milton is a writer who reflects habitually on his status as a writer, as in that auto-biographical digression in *The Reason of Church-Government* we examined in chapter 3. He is a writer who ensures that his books are in the big collections, which will in turn ensure their survival.[26] He is a writer who protests vehemently if he is misquoted even slightly, while mangling the texts of his enemies with utter disdain.[27] Whatever he may think of books in general (and Fish may well be right), Milton struggles to preserve and to defend books he himself has produced. For Milton, "freedom of publication" meant "freedom for Milton's publications."

The high rhetoric is probably just that, an attempt to involve his target readership, the lawmakers and opinion makers of London in the mid-1640s, in a heroic and elevated vision of the historical moment and their part in it. *Areopagitica* in a sense is his most rhetorical tract, the one that owes most to the methods of persuasion he had learned as part of his formal education, both in its shape and in the way it persistently works its audience. The great business of saving the lifeblood of master spirits is offered as a fit extension of Parliament's and London's larger heroic role as bulwark of the godly revolution:

> Behold now this vast City; a City of refuge, the mansion house of liberty, encompast and surrounded with his [God's] protection; the shop of warre hath not there more anvils and hammers waking, to fashion out the plates and instruments of armed Justice in defence of beleaguer'd

Truth, then there be pens and heads there, sitting by their studious lamps, musing, searching, revolving new notions and idea's wherewith to present, as with their homage and their fealty the approaching Reformation: others as fast reading, trying all things, assenting to the force of reason and convincement. What could a man require more from a Nation so pliant and so prone to seek after knowledge. What wants there to such a towardly and pregnant soile, but wise and faithfull labourers, to make a knowing people, a Nation of Prophets, of Sages, and of Worthies. We reck'n more then five months yet to harvest; there need not be five weeks, had we but eyes to lift up, the fields are white already. (*CPW,* II, 553–54)

London since 1642 had had a beleaguered air. Indeed, the royalist army had marched on the city only to turn back at Turnham Green, which lies between central London and what is now Heathrow airport. Royalists garrisoned the towns that controlled principal routes to London. But in 1644 the royalists drew back, for example, from Reading. Four months before *Areopagitica* was published, Parliament enjoyed at Marston Moor the first decisive victory of the war, destroying the royalist army of the North, and the tide of battle was running Parliament's way. Milton in his heroic vein taps London's sense of relief and optimism.

He plays Parliament itself with similar skill. *Areopagitica* attempts the most sustained *captatio benevolentiae* (or "the securing of goodwill from the audience") of any of his prose works, and the audience he woos in the opening paragraphs is explicitly Parliament, which needs some careful handling because his tract is both an indictment of its recent legislation and a request for its repeal. Hence Milton offers praise for "your milde and equall Government" as opposed to "that jealous hautinesse of Prelates and cabin Counsellours" (*CPW,* II, 488–89).

The tract also depends upon a powerful stratagem designed to manipulate the prejudices and concerns of a broad cross section of Parliamentary opinion, the widespread loathing of Catholicism. Thus it is that when Milton offers a historical account of the origins of licensing, he does so in terms that lay the innovation at the door of the Council of Trent, the ecumenical gathering that launched the Counter-Reformation against the Protestant Reformation of Northern Europe: "the Councell of Trent, and the Spanish Inquisition engendring together brought forth, or perfeted those Catalogues, and expurging Indexes that rake through the entralls of many an old good author, with a violation wors then any could be offer'd to his tomb" (*CPW,* II, 502–3); I wonder whether we are to recognize a point of connection, here, with the violation of Bucer's grave. The mechanisms of press control devised by Catholicism to combat Protestantism were then taken up by English bishops to resist the necessary secondary Reformation of the Church of England, in "gay imitation . . . apishly Romanizing" the legislation of England (*CPW,* II, 504–5). Milton thus involves the Laudian church with the church of Rome and implicates both in the origins of licensing as a mode of censorship. As an account, *Areopagitica* rests on some earlier narratives, but it is remote from the truth. Printing had been controlled in England since its inception, and all regimes from the Long Parliament through the various governmental manifestations of the English Republic favored licensing as a straightforward and effective mode of control. It is not singularly Catholic legislation.

Of Education

One tract of 1643–1645 stands apart from matters of divorce reform and the toleration of heterodox opinion: the eight-page open letter *Of Education. To Master* Samuel Hartlib, published in June 1644. We have no reason to suppose Milton had been in gainful employment as a schoolteacher, but he certainly was actively educating his two nephews, John and Edward Phillips, whom he took into his household in 1640, and at times he had other pupils. The pamphlet contributes to a debate currently stimulated by Hartlib, a polymath of Anglo-Polish ancestry currently living in London and much involved in numerous programs for scientific and educational reformation. It is clear that Milton writes at Hartlib's insistence after informal discussions about his educational theories; Hartlib has professed "satisfaction . . . from those incidentall discourses" and Milton can no longer resist his request (*CPW,* II, 363).

Milton is drawn, as if compulsively, to statements of high principle. Here, he explains that the larger end of education is to reverse what has been lost by the fall of Adam and Eve and the expulsion from the paradisal state:

> The end then of learning is to repair the ruins of our first parents by regaining to know God aright, and out of that knowledge to love him, to imitate him, to be like him, as we may the neerest by possessing our souls of true vertue, which being united to the heavenly grace of faith makes up the highest perfection. (*CPW,* II, 366–67)

Evidently, though, this restoration is not to be available to men without property or to women of any class, for Milton's academy, in this event, is a masculine institution designed to produce the ruling elite of a Puritan state:

> I call therefore a compleate and generous Education that which fits a man to perform justly, skilfully and magnanimously all the offices both private and publike of peace and war. (*CPW,* II, 377–79)

In the context of war, the products of his academy are to make up a cadre of officers; in the context of peace, they are to be masters of economic development (especially by improving agriculture), parliamentarians, and church leaders. The academy is to be in a "spatious house and ground about it," and its staff-student ratio is set at 1:6.5 (*CPW,* II, 379–80). Milton has nothing to say about funding.

In many ways Milton's vision is forward-looking, but what it looks forward to is the education of a privileged minority of Englishmen today, that combination of major public school (Eton, Harrow, and the like) and Oxbridge, restricted by the ability to pay and conducted in single-sex boarding institutions. Milton's scheme even corresponds to the projected age range for education, 12 years to 21 (*CPW,* II, 379). The Officer Training Corps is compulsory:

> about two hours before supper, they are by a sudden alarum or watch word, to be call'd out to their military motions, under skie or covert, according to the season, as was the Romane wont; first on foot, then as their age permits, on horse back, to all the art of cavalry; That having in sport, but with much exactnesse, and dayly muster, serv'd out the rudiments of their Souldiership in all the skill of embattailing, marching, encamping, fortifying, beseiging and battering, with all the helps of ancient and modern stratagems, *Tactiks* and warlike maxims, they may as it were out of a long warre come forth renowned and perfect Commanders in the service of their country. (*CPW,* II, 411–12)

Besides the cadet force, Milton insists on compulsory physical education; he particularly commends fencing and wrestling (*CPW,* II, 409). The academic component of the academy is as rigorously programmed and punctiliously required. He offers reading lists for several component disciplines; he attempts a timetable; not even Sunday is unprogrammed (Theology and Church History—*CPW,* II, 399).

Milton's dream academy may strike us as a version of hell: repressive, prescriptive, elitist, masculinist, militaristic, dustily pedantic, class-ridden, affectionless. It is hard to imagine it would be endured by anyone as instinctively oppositional as its designer. What remains of interest about the tract, though, relates to the critique it offers of Milton's own educational experience and to the disclosure it offers of his particular cultural assumptions and concerns.

Milton evidently thought that contemporary education spent far too much time teaching pupils to write in foreign tongues, especially Latin, and that the practice reflected a concern with how knowledge and ideas are expressed rather than with knowledge and ideas themselves. This notion found expression in the way he taught his nephews—we have their accounts of the experience—and it reflects the ideas of Francis Bacon, the greatest of English thinkers on the issues of the new science and its implications for education. For Bacon, the first distemper of learning was when "men study words and not matter."[28] Milton writes, "language is but the instrument convaying to us things usefull to be known" (*CPW,* II, 369). There is a purposeful functionalism to Milton's educational philosophy that he owes to Bacon.

Chapter Five
1649

On 30 January 1649, on a scaffold outside the Banqueting House in Whitehall, Charles I was beheaded, and England began its only experience of republican government.

When Milton published his final divorce tracts in 1645, he wrote from a position of weakness as an outsider to the realm of power. Both the divorce tracts and *Areopagitica* are consonant with at least a general alignment with Independency and with the toleration of a broad spectrum of opinion, and his impatience and irritation with Presbyterian and similar less radical and less tolerant Puritan tendencies are clear. Characteristically, though, he addressed his remarks to the Long Parliament and to the Westminster Assembly of Divines, both of which were controlled by people unsympathetic to his heterodoxy. No matter how eloquent his exposition, his chances of carrying such an audience with him were poor, nor did his work significantly impact upon political developments. Licensing was not relaxed; the divorce law was not reviewed.

No prose work is extant from 1646–1648, but the process of Milton's radicalization, of his recognition that Presbyterians are his enemies and retard the completion of the reformation along lines he advocated, finds expression in poems that have been tentatively attributed to this period, such as "On the New Forcers of Conscience under the Long Parliament":

> Because you have thrown off your prelate lord,
>   And with stiff vows renounced his liturgy
>   To seize the widowed whore plurality
>   From them whose sin ye envied, not abhorred,
> Dare ye for this adjure the civil sword
>   To force our consciences that Christ set free . . . ?[1]

Milton here draws a distinction between the role of the civil law in enforcing legislation necessary for social order and the operation of the conscience of each godly believer, which is of no concern to government. Such a separation was a central tenet of Independency, and it found a place in the political and spiritual consciousness of the powerful group in the higher echelon of Parliament's New Model Army of which Oliver Cromwell was the central figure. Milton trod a path well beaten by this cadre from root-and-branch antiepiscopalianism soft on sectaries to Independent tolerationism and thence to regicide.

The years of Milton's silence were years of Realpolitik between Parliament and the army. Charles I, utterly beaten from the battlefield, surrendered to the government of his Scottish kingdom in May 1646. The Scots handed him to the English Parliament in January 1647, but in June 1647 the army snatched him and he remained in their custody until his death. That event was a power play in the context of a protracted confrontation, which some historians later attributed at least as much to the material circumstances of the army as to ideological divisions.[2] Parliament owed the army £3 million in back pay—"this in the context of a kingdom whose royal revenues had never approached £1m p. a.[per year]"[3] Attempts to disband much of the army without making provision for settlement lent an air of industrial dispute to a conflict that ultimately focused on what should be done with the King. An army that had just won a civil war and that embodied a degree of military organization and competence without precedent in English history probably could not have been resisted as long as it remained cohesive. The Levelers, political radicals looking for the kind of revolution that would have enfranchised many more of the male population than before, became active among the rank and file and among more junior officers. But Cromwell and his group played them carefully, avoiding open conflict (and their subsequent suppression) until the confrontation with Parliament had been won. Against the New Model Army, Parliament had only the dubious resource of a rapidly reorganized London militia, and without significant difficulty the army occupied London in August 1647, the month after their seizure of the King.

A *modus vivendi* was temporarily established between Parliament and the army, but in the spring of 1648 a second civil war broke out as Charles I's Scottish kingdom, which had fought on the Parliamentary side in the first civil war, now invaded England in his defense and while royalist uprisings developed in several English regions. The New Model Army once more entered the field, and its commander-in-chief, Sir Thomas Fairfax, was the subject of a poem Milton presumably wrote shortly after Fairfax's recapture of Colchester in June 1648. The poem shows the new sense among whom we may now term "Revolutionary Independents"[4] that a final political settlement must be made that would finish both the bloody duplicity of Charles and the opportunism of the Long Parliament's Presbyterian ascendancy:

> O yet a nobler task awaits thy hand;
> For what can war, but endless war still breed,
> Till truth, and right from violence be freed,
> And public faith cleared from the shameful brand
> Of public fraud. In vain doth valour bleed
> While avarice, and rapine share the land.[5]

That new resolution soon found its expression in London politics, and in November 1648 the army laid before the House of Commons a demand that the King be brought to trial. In the 10 weeks between that date and the King's execution, the Cromwellian group ruthlessly drove matters forward:

> During that time an Army of 40,000 men, dominated by a resolute group of officers (chief among them Oliver Cromwell and his son-in-law Henry Ireton) took over the effective government of the country, purged and manipulated Parliament ["Pride's Purge," early in December, excluded members who would have opposed them], created the necessary revolutionary procedures to try the King, while suppressing other revolutionary motions not to their purpose, brought the King to judgment in Westminster Hall in defiance of almost all legal opinion, secured fifty-nine signatures to his death warrant, and an executioner to carry out the sentence, and finally proclaimed England a Republic.[6]

Milton, too, mounted this tiger of revolutionary change.

The Tenure of Kings and Magistrates

A fortnight after the execution of the King, there appeared *The Tenure of Kings and Magistrates*. It is more properly termed a regicide tract, justifying the killing of Charles I, rather than a republican tract, justifying the establishment of a new kind of government. We need not be surprised. England had no developed tradition of republican governmental theory. In the Elizabethan and Jacobean periods and throughout the rule of Charles I before 1640, the predominant political ideology had represented the monarch as a semimystical figure, uniquely privileged by God to govern the kingdoms of the British Isles. Alternative voices were not heard, and criticism of the monarch, even into the early and mid-

1640s, characteristically took the oblique line of criticizing, instead, the monarch's chief ministers.[7] The prosecution of Charles I was in a sense a continuation of the process of prosecuting allegedly bad ministers for particular malpractices that had begun with the trial and execution of Thomas Wentworth, Earl of Strafford, in 1641 and had continued with the trial and execution of William Laud, Archbishop of Canterbury, in 1645.

Indeed, Milton's February pamphlet looks backward to justify the actions of January rather than forward to the republican experiment. At the level of theory, it focuses on the rights of citizens to bring their kings to trial. Milton subscribes to a version of the social contract theory of government. He posits a vague prehistory to the contemporary state, in which free men (Milton's political analysis has no role for women) give up some part of their individual freedom in order to achieve the advantages of a stable society underwritten by the enforcement of law:

> No man who knows ought, can be so stupid to deny that all men naturally were borne free, being the image and resemblance of God himself, and were by privilege about all the creatures, born to command and not to obey: and that they liv'd so. Till from the root of *Adams* transgression, falling among themselves to doe wrong and violence, and foreseeing that such courses must needs tend to the destruction of them all, they agreed by common league to bind each other from mutual injury, and joyntly to defend themselves against any that gave disturbance or opposition to such agreement. Hence came Citties, Townes and Common-wealths. And because no faith in all was found sufficiently binding, they saw it needfull to ordaine som authoritie, that might restrain by force and punishment what was violated against peace and common right. This autoritie and power of self-defence and preservation being originally and naturally in every one of them, and unitedly in them all, for ease, for order, and least each man should be his own partial Judge, they communicated and deriv'd either to one, whom for the eminence of his wisdom and integritie they chose above the rest, or to more then one whom they thought of equal deserving: the first was call'd a King; the other Magistrates. (*CPW*, III, 198–99)

So the need for strong government has its origins in the fall of mankind and the legacy of original sin, which makes lives and property susceptible to crime unless social structures of a defensive nature are developed. Magistrates, who defend and enforce the laws, and monarchs, whose roles are analogous, derive their power from the choice of free citizens. The values inscribed in Milton's analysis are transparent. This is a patriarchal world view shaped by a concern with property and with the rights of property-owning males. It is premised on "that power, which is the root and sourse of all liberty, to dispose and *oeconomize* in the Land which God hath giv'n them, as Maisters of Family in thir own house and free inheritance" (*CPW,* III, 237).

Certain principles derive from the contract Milton postulates. Governmental systems are to serve the political nation, not the other way around, and "the people" (a difficult term for Milton in this as in his other political pamphlets) retain inalienable rights:

> It being . . . manifest that the power of Kings and Magistrates is nothing else, but what is only derivative, transferr'd and committed to them in trust from the People, to the Common good of them all, in whom the power yet remaines fundamentally, and cannot be tak'n from them, without a violation of thir natural birthright, and seeing that from hence *Aristotle* and the best of Political writers have defin'd a King, him who governs to the good and profit of his People, and not for his own ends, it follows from necessary causes, that the Titles of Sov'ran Lord, natural Lord, and the like, are either arrogancies, or flatteries. (*CPW,* III, 202)

Out of enlightened self-interest, the people adopted a monarchical system of government; that doesn't mean they have ceased to be free or that they have surrendered all dignity and all rights to the monarch. Note that Milton's political vision, although it rests on a contract theory, is informed by a sense of human values (especially of the value of men like himself, perhaps) and by an austere aesthetic that loathes the pomp and pageantry of royalism. Charles I was not the citizen's "Lord"; he was the citizen's employee, charged with responsibilities to serve the citizen and protect his property.

But the issue of property immediately resurfaces in another form. Royalist apologists argued that kings of England inherited absolute rights over their citizens. Milton seems unimpressed with the hereditary claims of kings—to him, that seems no more than a "courtesie or convenience" for transition from monarch to monarch. But he is adamant about what kings do inherit—it is not power over him and his like: "to say . . . the King hath as good right to his Crown and dignitie, as any man to his inheritance, is to make the Subject no better then the Kings slave, his chattell, or his possession that may be bought and sould" (*CPW,* III, 203). Such a notion of kingship cannot be reconciled to the inalienable rights of the property-owning citizen and to that dignity Milton claims.

That further royalist claim, that kings are accountable only to God, would render monarchs above the law. If they cannot be brought to account at the level of theory, then no bounds may be set to their power. They can do with people whatever their whim inclines them to do. Once more, the notion violates Milton's first principle about the contractual origins of government and outrages his sense of human worth (especially his own). This notion would allow the King to treat citizens as "so many beasts, or vermin under his Feet, not to be reasond with, but to be trod on," although among them may well be found "many thousand Men for wisdom, vertue, nobleness of mind, and all other respects, but the fortune of his dignity, farr above him" (*CPW,* III, 204–5). Milton knows himself to be smarter than Charles I was, to be more godly, and to possess a breadth of vision far greater (and later in 1649, in his *Eikonoklastes,* Milton gets his chance to prove it).

What follows most significantly from the contractual argument is the notion that kings may be subject to dismissal and accountability:

> It follows lastly, that since the King or Magistrate holds his autoritie of the people, both originaly and naturally for their good in the first place, and not his own, then may the people as oft as they shall judge it for the best, either choose him or reject him, retaine him or depose him though no Tyrant, meerly by the liberty and right of free born Men, to be govern'd as seems to them best. (*CPW,* III, 206)

Even good kings may be dismissed. Of course, all this talk of the powers of the people begs an important question: Who are the people? Obviously not women; in seventeenth-century England female emancipation was not yet an issue. But not all the men of England, either. Indeed, Milton's analysis is open to criticism from right and left. Presbyterians—the new Presbyterian royalists—could claim that the will of enfranchised Englishmen, those that satisfied the property qualification to vote, had found proper expression in the constitutionally elected Long Parliament. Its representivity had been compromised in 1642 when the King's supporters had withdrawn. It had been utterly vitiated by Colonel Pride's exclusion of those members disinclined to support the prosecution of the King. Milton in *The Tenure* attributes a lofty role to the will of the people, but his party has ruthlessly acted to ensure that that will, constitutionally expressed by the political nation in its election of Members of Parliament, was never allowed to secure the retention of monarchy in general and of Charles I in particular.

To the left of Revolutionary Independents were the Levelers. They, too, had a political model that foregrounded the role of the people. But for them all adult males that were not immediately dependent upon another, such as servants, or else dependent on charity, had a stake in the political life of England and should be allowed to vote in elections for a reformed parliament. The Leveler political platform found expression in a series of manifestos, the last of which, *An Agreement of the Free People of England* (May 1649), opens with this proposition:

> That the Supreme Authority of England and the Territories therewith incorporate, shall be and reside henceforward in a Representative of the People consisting of four hundred persons, but no more; in the choice of whom (according to naturall right) all men of the age of one and twenty yeers and upwards (not being servants, or receiving alms, or having served the late King in Arms or voluntary Contributions) shall have their voices; and be capable of being elected to that Supreme Trust, those who served the King being disabled for ten years onely.[8]

Perhaps one-sixth of the adult male population of England had been enfranchised to vote in the elections of 1640 that had returned the Long Parliament. Milton's political allies had narrowed further that representative structure, excluding those who would not support them against the King. The Levelers, led by John Lilburne and other radicals, sought to make Parliament representative of a far larger sector of the male population. Milton's own concerns with the rights of property and that class consciousness, pervasive in the prose but most sharply manifest in *Colasterion,* precluded political radicalism of the Leveler stamp. The regime he supports was forged, in effect, in a ruthless coup d'état, but those associated with it saw in its success its justification. It was a manifestation of God's providence toward his saints, of the work of "God out of his providence and high disposal" (*CPW,* III, 193). Those who had thus been given power were not in the business of turning it over to poor men to dispose of. The "people" in whose name Milton speaks in 1649 is a rather narrow subset of the population of England.

Who is Milton really trying to convince in *The Tenure?* In part, I suppose, so radical an action as regicide leaves even its proponents needing some reassurance about the appropriateness and legality of their actions. Severing the King's head severed connections with decades of English constitutional ideology, and the action left many of its supporters as perplexed as their opponents. As Blair Worden perceptively observes, "The regicide was not the fruit of republican theory. Most of its organisers were concerned to remove a particular king, not king-ship. They cut off King Charles' head and wondered what to do next."[9] Unlike several of the tracts of 1642–1645, *The Tenure* is not addressed to Parliament. What came to be known derogatorily as "the Rump Parliament" or simply "the Rump" (the part still sitting after Pride's Purge) may have needed reassurance, and *The Tenure* provides it, but it has another target readership. Those Englishmen who had been active against the King but who had refused at the last minute to stay the course had to be rendered at least neutral in the developing conflict between the New Model Army and the alliance of royalist forces still pursuing the Second Civil War. The newly royalist Presbyterians had to be reassured.

Milton was only partially adequate to the task; his own resentment of his treatment over the divorce tracts rankled too deeply for him to contain it. But he did what he could within the limitation imposed by his own savage pleasure in the political eclipse of enemies. There are three principal components to Milton's polemical strategy. First, he presupposes the most significant common ground between Presbyterians and Independents, namely, that Charles I was a man of blood responsible for the deaths and sufferings of the civil wars. Second, he rehearses the Presbyterians' (wholly acceptable) role in initiating and prosecuting the military conflict. He attempts to discredit the Presbyterian leadership with their supporters. Finally, he asserts that Presbyterians have nothing to fear from the Rump and everything to lose if Charles II is restored in place of his father. (Of course, royalists had immediately declared him King.)

Milton's case is not that Charles I was guilty as charged, but that Parliament had the right to prosecute him. Of course Charles was guilty— once brought to trial, the verdict would go necessarily against him. Once it had gone that far, he could not escape justice:

> what hath a native King to plead, bound by so many Covnants, benefits and honours to the welfare of his people, why he through the contempt of all Laws and Parlaments, the onely tie of our obedience to him, for his own wills sake, and a boasted prerogative unaccountable, after sev'n years warring and destroying of his best Subjects, overcom, and yeilded prisoner, should think to scape unquestionable, as a thing divine, in respect of whom so many thousand Christians destroy'd, should lie unaccounted for, polluting with their slaughterd carcasses all the Land over, and crying for vengeance against the living that should have righted them. (*CPW,* III, 214)

Rank-and-file supporters of the Presbyterian position could find much to sympathize with here. The King had duped them; he had broken agreements with them; he had led them on and let them down; and in the field of battle, his troops had killed their comrades. If they would not take that last step of making him answerable with his life for his conduct, some at least must have felt it not unwelcome that the Revolutionary Independents had followed the logic of the campaign against him to its grim conclusion.

For, indeed, Milton reminds them that the armies of Parliament tried hard enough, with Presbyterian support, to kill the King on the battlefield:

> Have they not levied all these Warrs against him . . . and giv'n Commission to slay where they knew his person could not be exempt from danger? And if chance or flight had not sav'd him, how oft'n had they killd him, directing thir Artillery without blame or prohibition to the very place where they saw him stand? . . . Have they not beseig'd him, & to thir power forbidd him Water and Fire, save what they shot against him to the hazard of his life? (*CPW,* III, 230–31)

Milton was well on his way to establishing the hypocrisy of a Presbyterian leadership that could launch such a war and now would wring its hands at the graveside of monarchy. But the vehemence of his attack threatened the coherence of his strategy. Presbyterianism was a political movement in which divines functioned as its most significant ideologues, and their principal concern was the establishment of a uniform state church with its orthodoxies enforced by the apparatuses of the state. In *The Tenure,* the clergy emerge as selfish, ruthless beasts, laying waste to the land in pursuit of their material interests, "rambling from Benefice to Benefice, like rav'nous Wolves seeking where they may devour the biggest" (*CPW,* III, 241). Milton's growing antipathy to a professional clergy funded by tithes is apparent enough in his strictures against "these Mercenary noisemakers" (*CPW,* III, 236), and the argument he constructs has a plausibility: the Presbyterian divines were all for the war against the King while they stood to advance their careers in livings vacated by expelled Laudian clergy; but now that their faction was in political eclipse, they had found a new affection for the late King, for his son, and for the rights and privileges of monarchy. While "pluralities greas'd them thick and deep, to the shame and scandal of Religion, more then all the Sects and Heresies they exclaim against," then "to fight against the Kings person . . . was good, was lawfull, was no resist-

ing of Superior powers." Now that there was no personal advantage in
that line, they argued from their pulpits that Charles I was "a lawfull
Magistrate, a Sovran Lord, the Lords anointed, not to be touch'd" (*CPW,*
III, 196–97).

Milton leaves the ordinary Presbyterian to work it out for himself,
albeit with pretty strong guidance from the author. After all, among
"the party calld Presbyterian" he knows many to be "good and faithfull
Christians, though misledd by som of turbulent spirit" (*CPW,* III, 238).
Such people have nothing to fear from the Rump. They may gather
themselves into churches with a presbyterian system of church government, and within that community they may require observance of whatever doctrine they collectively determine. What they may not do under
the Rump is "to affect rigor and superiority over men not under them"
(*CPW,* III, 238); that is, they may not require by law the conformity of
others with the principles they determine. So that central tenet that distinguished Independency from the majority of the Westminster Assembly of Divines in the early 1640s had been established by the coup d'état
that brought Charles I to trial. But Presbyterians were free to pursue
every other aspect of the established Presbyterian denominational principles, and the state would underwrite that freedom. But what if they
let Charles II in? Milton produces a series of historical analogues to their
position:

> Stories can informe them how *Christiern* the second, King of *Denmark* not
> much above a hundred yeares past, driv'n out by his Subjects, and
> receav'd againe upon new Oaths and conditions, broke through them all
> to his most bloody revenge; slaying his chief opposers when he saw his
> time, both them and thir children invited to a feast for that purpose.
> (*CPW,* III, 239–40)

And so Milton continues. This tract is a first airing of a polemical stratagem that will recur in *Eikonoklastes* and, in the twilight of the republic,
in *The Readie and Easie Way to Establish a Free Commonwealth*. Presbyterians may find much to dislike under the government of Revolutionary
Independents, but it compares very favorably with a counterrevolution-
ary terror unleashed by a restored monarch. "Cling to nurse for fear of
worse" is the phrase modern political commentators use to describe the
gambit.

When *The Tenure* first appeared, it ended in a rather self-indulgent
and slightly hysterical attack on the Presbyterian clergy, "these Pulpit-
firebrands," "the Ministers of Mammon instead of Christ" (*CPW,* III,

243, 242). When the tract was reissued in a second edition in 1650, Milton ended rather more subtly. Adopting the technique he had used in the conclusion to *Tetrachordon,* he wheels out a series of citations from founding fathers of the Protestant tradition—Luther, Zwingli, Calvin, Bucer, and so on—to confirm that writers dear to the Presbyterians have accepted the principle that ungodly monarchs may be deposed.

Observations

Milton's new status, spokesperson for those in power rather than appellant outsider, found expression in an official government appointment. Adapting earlier parliamentary institutions, the Rump Parliament established a Council of State, drawn from its ranks, to handle much of the business of government. This body, which was to be annually elected, contained many enthusiastic and active supporters of the execution of the King, and that group was singularly active in the meetings and deliberations of the Council.[10] On 13 March 1649 a working party was established, charged with the review of foreign alliances, and was immediately asked "to speake wth Mr. Milton to know whether he will be employed as Secretary for the fforeigne tongues, and to report to the Councell." Two days later his acceptance was reported and the appointment made.[11] Milton, at age 40, had for the first time a proper job.

The post carried responsibilities for the preparation of documents in Latin, the *lingua franca* of diplomatic relations, and for the translations into English of Latin correspondence to the Council; we shall consider Milton's role in the preparation of such "state papers" in chapter 8. Milton had published no Latin prose before his appointment, although presumably he had something of a reputation as a competent neo-Latinist (an attribute he would have shared with many educated contemporaries, although perhaps few of them would have been so readily complicit in the business of a regicide regime). However, his proven talent as polemicist in vernacular prose was soon drawn upon.

On 28 March 1649 he was instructed to "make some observations upon the Complicac[i]on of interest wch is now amongst the severall designers against the peace of the Comonwealth. And that it be made ready to be printed wth the papers out of Ireland wch the House hath ordered to be printed."[12] Despite the failure of the royalist uprising in England and Wales, the Second Civil War continued in Ireland and Scotland, and Cromwell and the New Model Army would have to deal with each in turn.

Recent events in Ireland had given considerable encouragement to the royalist cause. The population of Ireland consisted of three principal groups: the indigenous Irish people, who retained the Catholic religion; a sort of anglophile ascendancy, mostly communicants of the Protestant and episcopalian Church of Ireland, who made up the traditional elite through whom England's domination of the island was maintained; and fairly recent Protestant (and characteristically Presbyterian) settlers of English and Scottish origin, who had been encouraged to emigrate to Ireland to establish a solid yeomanry sympathetic to English control and hostile to the Catholic majority. Ireland had been at war since the Catholic uprising of 1641. Charles I had supposedly sought to suppress this uprising through the agency of the Marquis of Ormonde, his Lord Lieutenant and a member of that episcopalian, anglophile elite, although it became clear that the notion was entertained that a Catholic army, levied in Ireland, could be usefully employed on the royalists' side in the First Civil War, and some regiments were sent over. But Baron Inchiquin, like Ormonde an Irish Protestant aristocrat, campaigned more vigorously throughout the 1640s against the Catholic confederacy (the "confederacy of Kilkenny").

The complex and very bloody civil war in Ireland, punctuated by occasional cessations of hostility, had seemingly been ended by agreements Ormonde entered into with the Catholics of the confederacy and with the Presbyterians, who were evidently prepared to accept the claims of Charles II. The royalists controlled all of Ireland and all the various armies in Ireland except for Dublin, held for Parliament by Colonel Michael Jones, and some northern coastal enclaves held by Colonel George Monck, all of which were under threat. Ormonde had at his disposal his own forces, Inchiquin's ruthless and successful Protestants, the Scottish Presbyterian Army of Ulster, and the troops of the Catholic confederacy.[13] Milton's pamphlet was commissioned in the context of this considerable crisis.

The pamphlet that resulted in May 1649 from the Council of State's instructions to Milton is *Articles of Peace, made and concluded with the Irish Rebels, and Papists, by James Earle of Ormond, for and in behalfe of the late King, and by verture of his autoritie. Also a Letter sent by Ormond to Col. Jones, Governour of Dublin, with his Answer thereunto. And A Representation of the Scotch Presbytery at Belfast in Ireland. Upon all which are added Observations.* It does not carry Milton's name, but it is endorsed "Publisht by Autority." Its status as an official government publication is evident and proclaimed.

Superficially, it is a curious document. Forty-four of its 65 pages are taken up not with Milton's prose but with the reproduction of the documents and declarations detailed on the title page. Two-thirds of the publication are given over as a platform to the enemies of the state that had promoted its production. But the Long Parliament had seen some years earlier the advantages of this polemical stratagem in the publication of *The Kings Cabinet Opened: or Certain Packets of Secret Letters Papers, Written with the Kings Own Hand, and Taken in His Cabinet at Nasby-Field, June 14, 1645* (London, 1645). This publication was also largely made up of documentation from enemy sources (in this case, letters taken from the private files of Charles I captured after the battle of Naseby), followed by "Annotations" from government civil servants pointing up what those documents disclose. In each case, what is disclosed is Stuart duplicity and a preparedness to cut deals with Catholics to advance the royalist cause against the interests of Protestants. As I have remarked elsewhere,[14] "The same strategy underpins the whole conception of *Observations*: a reading public, conditioned to interpret evidence of royalist and papist conspiracies, is presented once more with documentation of the same readiness of the Stuarts, in the words of the preface to *The Kings Cabinet,* to assail the godly English with 'all the Papists in *Europe* almost, especially the bloody Tygers of *Ireland.*' "

This tract plays on loathing of Catholicism in general and Irish Catholicism in particular in order to legitimize the regicide regime in the eyes of a broad spectrum of English Protestants. The intolerance it expresses and the violence it justifies make it a difficult pamphlet for a modern reader, for it is surely the ideological precursor of Cromwell's massacres of the populations of Drogheda and Wexford and of the whole ruthless and brutal campaign that substantially expropriated the ancestral homelands of the Catholic population of Ireland. It is not merely an intolerant tract; it is racist and imperialist.

Milton, however, uses an extant hatred; he does not invent it. There are two components to the immediate history of this hatred. Anti-Catholic sentiment had been an avenue of oppositionalism available since the Elizabethan period to those of a Puritan leaning who could not openly criticize the secular or religious ascendancy. This sentiment had a value, too, for those who wanted to maximize the common ground within English Protestantism, in that it defined Protestantism, uncontroversially, in terms of what it was not and supplied an object of hatred about the horrors of which all Protestants could agree. Peter Lake, whose shrewd analysis informs these comments, observes that "Popery

. . . became a unifying 'other' in the presence of which all those not directly implicated in the problem (popery) became part of the solution (non-popery)."[15] Recently, popery had become a convenient and plausible charge to level against some elements of the court of Charles I, whose Catholic queen could certainly be represented as a patroness of English Catholicism, but the issue would not have been raised if there had not already been a secure tradition of anti-Catholic sentiment on which to build.

The second element determining the foregrounding of this prejudice in the *Observations* related specifically to Ireland. Irish Catholics had fought on the side of Charles I, and a persistent anxiety existed that many more would be recruited to fight for his son. But more significantly still, since 1641 numerous vivid accounts had been published of the sufferings of Protestant coreligionists at the hands of the Irish Catholic "rebels." In the intervening centuries considerable historical effort has been invested in refuting or substantiating the horror stories and the body count. We have no reason to suppose that those newsbooks that so shocked the English nation were regarded as anything other than true by Milton and by the overwhelming majority of English Protestants who thought about such things. Distasteful though it may be, the modern reader really must look at such texts to reach an appropriate understanding of Milton's polemic. Consider these examples from the wholly typical *Remonstrance of the Barbarous Cruelties and Bloudy Murders Committed By the Irish Rebels Against the Protestants in Ireland . . . Being the examinations of many who were eye-witnesses of the same . . . Presented to the whole kingdome of England, that thereby they may see the Rebels inhumane dealings, prevent their pernicious practises, relieve their poore brethrens necessities, and fight for their Religions, Laws, and Liberties* (London, 1644), by Thomas Morley:

> *Grizell Maxwell* being in child (the child halfe borne, halfe unborne) they stript her starke naked, and drove her about an Arrows flight to the water and drowned her.
>
> The like they did to another English woman in the same parish in the beginning of the rebellion; which was little inferiour (if not more unnaturall and barbarous[)] then the rosting of Mr. *Watson* the minister alive after they had cut a collop out of either buttocke. . . .
>
> The rebels would send their children abroad in great troupes . . . armed with long wattles and whips, who would therewith beate mens privy members untill they beat or rather threshed them off, and then they woulde returne in great joy to their parents, who received them for such good service, as it were in triumph.

If any women were found dead, lying with their faces downward, they would turn them upon their backes, . . . censuring all parts of their bodies, but especially such as are not to be named; which afterwards they abused in so many waies and so filthily, as chaste eares would not endure the very naming thereof. . . .

A young fat Scotchman was murthered, and the Rebels made Candles of his grease.

They took another Scotchman and ripped up his belly, that they might come to his small guts. The one end whereof they tied to a Tree, and made him go round untill he had drawne them all out of his body. They then saying, they would try whether a dog, or a Scotchmans guts were longer.[16]

The components of these horrors, to a more skeptical age, seem perhaps contrived. Female humiliation and mutilation, atrocities on the unborn child, cannibalism, castration, necrophilia, and sadism of a Satanic ingenuity—here are all the elements necessary to identify the Irish Catholics as inhumane monsters, intractable to salvation, unworthy of correction, open only to ruthless and condign punishment. (But we should beware too readily discounting all such narratives as a perverse and tendentious construct; the documented horrors of our own century may not be thus conjured away.)

Milton was writing to people who had read these accounts and believed them. Never before had he been in so strong a polemical position. The documents demonstrated that Ormonde and the Scottish Presbyterians in Ulster were already in league with the Irish Catholics; the justification of the invasion was virtually self-evident:

> As for these Articles of Peace made with those inhumane Rebels and Papists of *Ireland* by the late King, as one of his last Masterpieces, We may be confidently perswaded, that no true borne *English-man,* can so much as barely reade them without indignation and disdaine, that those bloudy Rebels, and so proclaim'd and judg'd of by the King himself, after the mercilesse and barbarous Massacre of so many thousand *English,* (who had us'd their right and title to that Countrey with such tendernesse and moderation, and might otherwise have secur'd themselvs with ease against their Treachery) should be now . . . rewarded with . . . freedomes and enlargements . . . (*CPW,* III, 301)

But a more important (albeit seemingly secondary) objective was available, to demonstrate that the regicide government defended the national interest and that the Presbyterian leadership was prepared to jeopardize it for factional gain.

Indeed, although the document from the Presbytery of Belfast is considerably shorter than the Articles of Peace, Milton spends markedly longer "observing" on it. The alliance between the government of Scotland and the Long Parliament, which had proved the basis for Scotland's military involvement on the parliamentary side in the First Civil War, was the Solemn League and Covenant, which had included a clause that pointed to the establishment of a reformation of the Church of England to achieve, with the Scottish Presbyterian church, "the nearest conjuction and uniformity in religion, confession of faith, form of Church government, directory for worship and catechising," exactly the kind of uniformity that congregational Independency rejected, and a clause committing them "to preserve and defend the King's Majesty's person and authority."[17] Of course, the Solemn League and Covenant was a document from very early in the conflict with the King, marked with the necessary oblique formulas of that time. But the document left the regicide regime open to the frequently reiterated charge that it had broken the covenant. Milton picks the charge up and hurls it back:

> now they have joyn'd interest with the *Irish Rebels,* who have ever fought against the *Covnant.* . . . But as it is a peculiar mercy of God to his people, while they remain his, to preserve them from wicked confederations: so it is a mark and punishment of hypocrites to be drivn at length to mix thir cause, and the interest of thir *Covnant* with Gods enemies. (*CPW,* III, 325)

So much for Presbyterian scruples about the contract of 1643; the contract of 1649 brings them into league with Catholics who have already perpetrated the most abhorrent atrocities on Protestants.

It matters hugely that Milton takes issue with spokespersons, not of the English settlement in Ireland, but of the Scottish. Presbyterian Scotland was currently in arms against the regicide regime and had accepted Charles II as its King. (Cromwell was to settle with them after he had finished with Ireland.) Milton in the *Observations* purports to speak for England, to articulate English interests against the depredations of those other peoples who share the British Isles. That the Irish Catholics are savages is a point made frequently. He is at pains to demonstrate, too, the effeteness of the aristocracy, represented by Ormonde, and the obscurity, the marginality, of the Scottish Presbyterians. Ormonde's hereditary status is as a defender of the English interest in Ireland, a task he and his ancestors have assumed. But it is a minor role in an outpost of empire, and one often ineffectually discharged; it will not stand comparison with the achievements of Cromwell, the true servant of the commonwealth:

> *Cromwell* whom he [Ormonde] couples with a name of scorne, hath done in few yeares more eminent and remarkable Deeds whereon to *found* Nobility in his house, though it were wanting, and perpetuall Renown to posterity, then *Ormond* and all his Auncestors put together can shew from any record of thir *Irish* exploits, the widest scene of thir glory. (*CPW,* III, 312)

Milton portrays the Presbyterians as mean-minded, ignorant, idle men, railing at the might of a revived England from their "barbarous nook of *Ireland*" (*CPW,* III, 327). But the worst culprit is the dead King, whose final significant act has been, in effect, to give away an English possession in the "utter alienating and acquitting the whole Province of *Ireland* from all true fealty and obedience to the Common-wealth of *England*" (*CPW,* III, 305). Charles I gave Ireland away; Cromwell will get it back, just as Cromwell, in due course, will protect England from a Scottish incursion. Any Englishman with a sense of the *national* interest and a concern for his own property really has no choice but to let the new regime get on with the business of protecting both.

John Buchan, in his hagiographical biography of Cromwell, with evident disappointment concluded, "Oliver's Irish campaign is admittedly the chief blot on his fame," in that, although what he did at Drogheda and Wexford reflected contemporary beliefs and practices, "he must be judged by other standards."[18] Miltonists have shown a singular reluctance to consider in detail Milton's own "Irish expedition." In our own age, still riven centuries later by the sectarian conflicts seeded in the bloody events of 1641 and 1649, we surely have a responsibility to look clear-eyed at the *Observations,* however embarrassing to Milton's own hagiographers. Too many have been killed or maimed for us to look away.

Eikonoklastes

Milton's third and final tract of 1649, like the *Observations,* is a response on behalf of the government: *Eikonoklastes in Answer to a Book Intitl'd Eikon Basilike, The Portrature of his Sacred Majesty in his Solitudes and Sufferings.* We do not know exactly who commissioned him or when the instruction came, but he makes it clear in the *captatio benevolentiae* that this is something he has written out of duty rather than volition: "I take it on me as a work assign'd rather, then by me chos'n or affected. Which was the cause both of beginning it so late, and finishing it so leasurely, in the midst of other imployments and diversions" (*CPW*, III, 339). Perhaps we may take this at face value, although I suspect we would be ingenuous to do so. Milton had sought a worthy enemy since the inception of his career as polemicist. He was the man who had assailed Bishop Hall, but ended up embroiled in debate with the anonymous Modest Confuter of his *Animadversions*. He was the man who had tried to launch a great debate about divorce reform, but had found himself taking a petty lawyer to task in *Colasterion*. But *Eikon Basilike* was or purported to be written by the King himself. When Milton took it on, he did so on behalf of his political faction; but he did so in his own name: "I shall make no scruple to take up (for it seems to be the challenge both of him and all his party) to take up this Gauntlet, though a Kings, in the behalf of Libertie, and the Common-wealth" (*CPW*, III, 338). In a sense, this was the fight he had been looking for since *Of Reformation*. *Eikon Basilike* first appeared in February 1649; *Eikonoklastes,* in October. Perhaps Milton had indeed taken a long time to finish it because it was uncongenial work and he had other commitments. But it is a very long book by the standards of Civil War polemic, and, at 242 quarto pages, it is by far his longest vernacular exercise in the genre. No wonder it took a busy man with fading eyesight seven months to write it. The *Observations* had appeared as an anonymous government publication; *Eikonoklastes* carries on its title page the initials "J. M." There is a corporate idiom about the former; the latter is presented ultimately as a personal statement.[19] The gauntlet is taken up, and the conflict is single combat.

More acutely than for any other of Milton's works, it is important to set *Eikonoklastes* in its polemical context. The book it confronts stands outside the mainstream of the genre, distinguished by its idiom and its reception as much as by its apparent author. *Eikon Basilike* appeared in legions of editions, some 35 in 1649, with many more later, including translations. The book was keenly felt to threaten the version of events authorized by the new republic. Its very title, stressing that it is a portrait of his majesty, metaphorically appends the potency of a visual image of monarchy to a verbal appeal. Many editions carried a symbolic engraving, depicting Charles I at prayer, looking to accept Christ's crown of thorns and discarding his earthly crown. Copies of *Eikon Basilike* are common in research collections of early modern books. Some editions, no doubt, never had this frontispiece; but I strongly suspect that many of the copies that lack it now do so because it was removed for domestic display by original purchasers. Portraits meant rather more in the early modern period than they do in Western societies in our own age. Displaying them was a gesture of fealty. John Peacock, who has fascinatingly explored political portraiture, draws on the account of the contemporary Venetian ambassador, to observe that the change of dynasty from Tudor to Stuart occasioned a change in the pictures on domestic walls:

> Everywhere, Scaramelli [the Venetian ambassador] added, portraits of Elizabeth were being put away, and those of Mary Queen of Scots [mother of James I] displayed instead. . . . It seems clear enough that the people who had the motives and resources to switch their portraits—courtiers, government servants, substantial citizens—were signifying their readiness to co-operate with the new regime. The portraits of Mary were in themselves powerful signs of political docility.[20]

Charles I's concern with fashioning an image of himself as potent monarch found expression in his assembly at Whitehall of a cluster of stunning portraits of himself, preeminently by Van Dyck, as part of his fine personal collection. As early as 1644, Parliament's agents had purged that collection.[21] But now, posthumously, Charles had occasioned the production of an engraved portrait to hang on every supporter's wall as well as of a literary icon of himself. Far from indicating docility, the portraits indicated defiant noncollaboration with the republican regime. His was a difficult ghost for Parliament to exorcise.

Moreover, *Eikon Basilike* was a difficult target to hit. The book itself does not even look like a political tract. Most editions were in the smaller octavo format, usually used for prayer-books, personal bibles, and books of personal devotion, rather than the larger quarto format that characterized most of the tracts and newsbooks of the time. What you got when you bought it, besides the portrait, was a neat little book you could tuck in a pocket and ponder in private. It was a book you could carry around. Just owning it, having it, meant that in a sense you hadn't sold out.

The invitation to private contemplation curiously involves the reader in a shared activity. The title's reference to "His Sacred Maiestie in his Solitudes and Sufferings" implies the setting for its composition. Like the image of the lonely praying King in the frontispiece, the title suggests that this is a work of sadness, wrung from the captive King's lonely soul in the dark midnight of the royalist cause. The reader can share that act of contemplation and, like the martyr-king, rise stronger from it.

Each chapter of *Eikon Basilike* deals with an incident or episode from the recent history of England. Significantly, the book begins with the calling of the Long Parliament. All Charles's acts of overreaching and miscalculation that occasioned the crisis of 1637 and the catastrophe of the Scottish campaign are passed over. Likewise, the larger arguments against the conduct of the personal rule of Charles I are excluded. This is a text of extraordinary vagueness. For something that purports to be a narrative of events, it never descends from cloudy generalization to specific detail. Very few people are mentioned by name or title. Besides the King himself, only the queen, the Prince of Wales, Strafford (died 1641), and Sir John Hotham (died 1645) are thus identified. None of Charles's living adversaries is named, and although the book contains much talk of his "enemies" and of their "malice," the reader is uncertain as to whom he means. This vagueness is not mere chance. The royalists through 1647–1648 had been well aware of the divisions on the Parliamentarian side and had sought to exploit them. By naming no one, *Eikon Basilike* leaves open the possibilities of a deal with English Presbyterians analogous to those deals struck with Irish and Scottish Presbyterians. More surprising (and frustrating, from Milton's point of view), each chapter ends with a prayer, usually with some oblique relevance to the rest of the chapter. It is easy enough to deny facts and refute argument; but *Eikon Basilike* has few facts, and its argument is unsustained, and worse still, it is quite impossible to refute a prayer.

To see the full extent of Milton's problems, consider a chapter from the King's book. I have selected one of the shorter ones, "3. Upon His Majesties going to the House of Commons." It deals with the events of 4 January 1642. On 3 January, Charles had instructed the Lords to arrest one member and the Commons to arrest five prominent members of the opposition to the King, John Pym, John Hampden, William Strode, Denzil Holles, and Sir Arthur Haselrig. The Lords declined to do so but established a committee of enquiry; the Commons also declined, but responded that they would take care that their members answered the charge against them. The next day, the five members took their place, but word was received that the King was poised to march on Parliament and arrest them (the palaces of Whitehall and Westminster are adjacent). The members hurriedly left Westminster for the safety of the city of London just as the King and an armed troop, variously put at between 300 and 500 men, entered Parliament to effect the arrest. Charles displaced the speaker of the House of Commons from his chair, demanded the five members, realized they were no longer there, and uttered perhaps his only memorable speech, "Well, since I see all my birds are flown, I do expect from you [the House of Commons, or perhaps just the speaker of the House] that you will send them unto me as soon as they return hither . . . otherwise I must take my own course to find them."[22]

Here is Charles's version:

> My going to the House of Commons to demand Justice upon the 5 Members, was an act, which My enemies loaded with all the obloquies and exasperations they could.
>
> It filled indifferent men with great jealousies and feares; yea, and many of My friends resented it as a motion rising rather from Passion then Reason, and not guided with such discretion, as the touchinesse of those times required.
>
> But these men knew not the just motives, and pregnant grounds, with which I thought my self so furnished, that there needed nothing to such evidence, as I could have produced against those I charged, save only a free and legal Triall, which was all I desired.
>
> Nor had I any temptation of displeasure, or revenge against those mens persons, further then I had discovered those (as I thought) unlawfull correspondencies they had used, and engagements they had made, to embroyle my Kingdomes: of all which I missed but little to have produced writings under some mens own hands, who were the chief contrivers of the following Innovations.
>
> Providence would not have it so, yet I wanted not such probabilities as were sufficient to raise jealousies in any Kings heart, who is not wholly stupid and neglective of the publick peace, which to preserve by calling in Question half a dozen men, in faire and legall way (which God knowes was all my design) could have amounted to no worse effect, had it succeeded, then either to do Me, and my Kingdom right, in case they had been found guilty; or else to have cleared their Innocency, and removed my suspicions; which, as they were not raised out of any malice, so neither were they in Reason to be smothered.
>
> What flames of discontent this sparke (which I sought by all speedy and possible meanes to quench it) soon kindled, all the world is witnesse: The aspersion which some men cast upon that action, as if I had designed by force to assault the House of Commons, and invade their priviledge, is so false, that as God best knows, I had no such intent; so none that attended could justly gather from any thing I then said, or did, the least intimation of any such thoughts.
>
> That I went attended with some Gentlemen, as it was no unwonted thing for the Majesty and safety of a King so to be attended, especially in

discontented times; so were my followers at that time short of my ordinary Guard, and no way proportionable to hazard a tumultuary conflict. Nor were they more scared at my comming, then I was un-assured of not having some affronts cast upon me, if I had none with me to preserve a reverence to me; For many people had (at that time) learned to think those hard thoughts, which they have since abundantly vented against Me, both by words and deeds.

The summe of that businesse was this.

Those men, and their adherents were then looked upon by the affrighted vulgar, as greater protectors of their Lawes and Liberties, then my self, and so worthier of their protection. I leave them to God, and their own Consciences, who, if guilty of evill machinations; no present impunity, or popular vindications of them will be subterfuge sufficient to rescue them from those exact Tribunalls.

To which, in the obstructions of Justice among men, We must religously appeal, as being an argument to us Christians of that after unavoidable judgment, which shall re-judge what among men is but corruptly decided, or not at all.

I endeavoured to have prevented, if God had seen fit, those future Commotions, which I fore-saw, would in all likelyhood follow some mens activity (if not restrained) and so now hath done to the undoing of many thousands, the more is the pity.

But to over-awe the freedome of the Houses, or to weaken their just Authority by any violent impressions upon them, was not at all My designe: I thought I had so much Justice and Reason on My side, as should not have needed so rough assistance; and I was resolved rather to bear the repulse with patience, than to use such hazardous extremities.

But thou, O Lord, art My Witnesse in Heaven, and in My Heart: If I have purposed any violence or oppression against the Innocent: or if there were any such wickednesse in My thoughts.

Then let the enemy persecute My soule, and tread my life to the ground, and lay mine Honour in the dust.

Thou that seest not as man seeth, but lookest beyond all popular appearances, searching the heart, and trying the reines, and bringing to light the hidden things of darknesse, shew they selfe.

Let not my afflictions to esteemed (as with wise and godly men they cannot be) any argument of my sinne, in that matter; more then their Impunity among good men is any sure token of their Innocency.

But forgive them wherein they have done amisse, though they are not punished for it in the world.

Save thy servant from the privy conspiracies and open violence of bloudy and unreasonable men, according to the uprightnesse of my heart and the innocency of my hands in this matter.

Plead my cause, and maintain my right, O thou that sittest in the Throne, judging rightly, that thy Servant may ever rejoice in thy salvation.[23]

About a later chapter, Milton complains that Charles used "the plausibility of large and indefinite words, to defend himself at such a distance as may hinder the eye of common judgement from all distinct view & examination of his reasoning" (*CPW*, III, 456–57). Milton's point holds good for the whole of *Eikon Basilike*, in which the author habitually reflects with a lofty vagueness that makes the specific details and the logical process difficult to bring to scrutiny. Chapter 3 shows most of the polemical repertoire so distinctive of *Eikon Basilike*.[24] Charles is represented not as someone responding ineptly to a complex political situation but rather as a heroic battler against a natural disaster, attempting to "quench" the sparks of rebellion before they can "kindle" a worse disaster. How have his actions been misrepresented? By the malice of unnamed "enemies," who have loaded the act "with all the obloquies and exasperations they could." But what was the act really like? Well, it involved going to Parliament "with some Gentlemen." Why had he failed? Not through incompetence, you understand, or the quick-witted courage of the Parliamentarians opposed to the King and their supporters in the City. No, it was "Providence," that enigmatic divine process that required from England a period of penitential suffering. And the King's response to the setback? More sadness than anger, a meditation on "the pity" that he could not, thus, avoid the bloodshed of the Civil War. Time for a prayer.

Milton's response is essentially one of supplementation and redefinition. Where there is vagueness, he brings precision; where there is an aloof gloss, he brings a different, sharper interpretation. Persistently, his tactic is to involve the reader in comparing the King's version of events against what the reader already knows or believes. Milton's intended audience is not old royalists—they can only be beaten in the field by the New Model Army and intimidated into compliance. He wants to remind former allies, Presbyterians and those close to them, of what really happened in the years before the alliance against the King crumbled. The House of Commons that Charles invaded was full, for the most part, not of Independents but of Presbyterians. Of the five members involved in the event, Pym, Hampden, and Strode were dead, Holles had developed into a leader of the Presbyterian group in Parliament, and only Haselrig supported the republic. So here Milton's objective, if he remains focused, can be accomplished. First some details: the very door of Parliament was kept open and all the passageways were filled with "about three hunderd Swaggerers and Ruffians, who but expected, nay audibly call'd for the word of onset to beginn a slaughter" (*CPW*, III, 377). "Audibly"—Milton deals in facts, what was heard, what was noted, what was reported immediately after the event. The charge against the five members was that they were in correspondence with the Scots to bring them in against the King; Milton rehearses the well-established argument that Charles was in negotiation to bring in Catholic armies from France and Ireland (*CPW*, III, 377–78). So Charles says he had not intended an assault on the House of Commons; Milton juxtaposes Charles's later statement "that *any course of violence had bin very justifiable.*" So "we may then guess how farr it was from his designe" (*CPW*, III, 379). Note that use of "we"; Milton is incorporating his readership in this examination of evidence.

Charles's phrase about going to the House of Commons "attended with some Gentlemen" implies a kind of civility, of order, of ceremony even; once more, Milton brings the vague grandeur of the locution into touch with Parliament's accepted account of events:[25]

> Gentlemen indeed; the ragged Infantrie of Stewes and Brothels; the spawn and shipwrack of Taverns and Dicing Houses: and then he pleads *it was no unwonted thing for the Majesty and safety of a King to be so attended, especially in discontented times.* An illustrious Majestie no doubt, so attended: a becomming safety for the King of *England,* plac'd in the fidelity of such Guards and Champions: Happy times; when Braves and Hacksters, the onely contented Members of his Goverment, were thought the fittest and the faithfullest to defend his Person against the discontents of a Parlament and all good Men. (*CPW*, III, 380–81)

"All good men": Milton moves to incorporate the Presbyterians back into the alliance that had been obtained in 1642. Persistently, he seeks out the knowledge, beliefs, and prejudices shared by a broad spectrum of Puritan opinion. The whole passage reanimates a time-worn stereotype of the pox-ridden, debt-ridden, drunken and licentious Cavalier, the bugbear that strides through the Parliamentarians' newsbooks of 1642–1645.[26]

The argument about Providence is pulled into shape as a justification for Parliament's conduct. God protected them; God brought them to success; God watched over them as the King was brought to trial. The King calls on "Gods Tribunal"; through his ill fate we may "behold God hath judg'd, and don to him in the sight of all men according to the verdict of his own mouth" (*CPW,* III, 381). Milton's chapter ends in grim contemplation of a divine justice manifest in the undoing of the King: "God and his judgements have not bin mock'd" (*CPW,* III, 382). A people—one whose political consciousness had been shaped for decades by the notion that the King is the Lord's anointed, protected by him and secured in his privileges by the force of divine right—now faced the simple truths, either that God did not protect kings or that God had permitted this King to be brought to punishment.

Milton does not engage the prayer that concluded chapter 3 of *Eikon Basilike,* and generally it is his policy to leave them well alone, as he puts it a little later, "With his Orisons I meddle not, for he appeals to a high Audit" (*CPW,* III, 405). Milton has to turn the King's extraordinary book into an ordinary one, another partisan account of the origins and conduct of the Civil War, which can then be brought up against a different version of reality, one that most Puritans would share. Meddling with the prayers in a systematic way would divert him from that objective.

What Milton does with chapter 3 of *Eikon Basilike* is repeated endlessly throughout *Eikonoklastes,* as he "walk[s] side by side" with the King, opposing lofty fantasy with Puritan hard facts. It is an extraordinarily controlled performance. Very rarely does Milton cut loose with those vivid similes and metaphors that so enlivened *Of Reformation* or *Areopagitica.* Indeed, part of the larger argument of *Eikonoklastes* is that *Eikon Basilike* violates decorum by bringing an inappropriate poetical floweriness to the discourse of politics. For example, after quoting one singularly obtrusive simile from *Eikon Basilike,* Milton gravely comments,

> Poets indeed use to vapor much after this manner. But to bad Kings, who without cause expect future glory from thir actions, it happ'ns as to bad Poets; who sit and starve themselves with a delusive hope to win immortality by thir bad lines. (*CPW,* III, 502)

Milton could scarcely reach for his own singing robes while sustaining this critique.

Eikonoklastes has attracted little enthusiasm in modern criticism. It avoids large liberal principles; it is fine-grained and studiedly unflamboyant; it attacks a King and justifies a fairly dubious legal process that resulted in an act of capital punishment. But for me, it is Milton's prose masterpiece, his most sustained tract, his most careful and his most responsible. Readers will point out that *Eikonoklastes* "failed" in its objective of destroying the sympathetic image of King Charles the Martyr, kept in "the people's" hearts until the Restoration of his son in 1660. Perhaps so; but the tract made its own contribution to the real and immediate success of the Rump Parliament in securing the acquiescence of Presbyterian former allies to the process of republican government. In 1651, when Charles II entered England at the head of a predominantly Scottish army, to his surprise very few English Presbyterian royalists went to join him. That lack of following was the product of many elements—of the Rump's skillful courting of moderate opinion through rather conservative government, no doubt also of the sense of the power of the New Model Army. But Milton's tracts of 1649, and preeminently *Eikonoklastes,* made their contribution to that process of assuring all the godly that a Stuart king was still their common enemy. In defense of the republic Milton did what he could, and in *Eikonoklastes* he did it with consummate accomplishment.

Chapter Six

The Latin *Defenses* of the English Republic

Milton's first publications on behalf of the English republic were both in English, although his primary responsibilities as a public servant related to his skills as a Latinist. His three remaining publications in his capacity of state employee were all in Latin.

Toward the end of 1649 there appeared a royalist book potentially as damaging as *Eikon Basilike* titled *Defensio regia pro Carolo ad Serenissumum Magnae Britanniae regem Carolum II. Filium natu majorem, Heredem successoreum legitimum* [*The Royal Defense of Charles I to the most serene king Charles II, his eldest son by birth, his heir, and his legitimate successor*]. The title page is endorsed *"Sumptibus Regiis," "at royal expense,"* for this is a work as acknowledgedly official as *Eikonoklastes* had been. The book lists no place of publication, although clearly it was published in Amsterdam, and although it appeared anonymously, its author was widely known to be Claude de Saumaise ("Claudius Salmasius" in the Latinized form), a French Protestant academic and divine with an international reputation for his erudition. According to Parker, "By common acclaim, Salmasius was one of the three or four greatest living scholars in the whole of Europe." In the manner of academic superstars of the European Renaissance, he had been invited to settle in several countries, and since 1631 he had resided in Leyden.[1]

The book plainly presented the new republic with serious public relations problems. Aimed at a Continental European readership, it was calculated to make difficulties for the regime in normalizing its diplomatic connections with the other states of Europe. Walter Strickland, the English republic's agent in the Hague, had been monitoring Salmasius's progress with the commission to write his royalist tract and had acted to persuade the Dutch authorities, with some initial success, to prohibit its printing, although by 1652 it had gone through more than a dozen editions. Although the republican regime acted to limit importation of the book into England, it was much more difficult to mitigate its Continental influence.

With hindsight, a twentieth-century Miltonist may well feel it wholly appropriate that the Council of State should have decided on 8 January 1650 "That M[r] Milton doe prepare something in answer to the Booke of Saltmatius, and when hee hath done itt bring itt to the Councell."[2] I cannot imagine, however, that the step was taken with perfect equanimity. Milton was being matched against a genuine heavyweight. In 1650, Milton was a minor poet (his early verse had appeared in his first collection in 1645, most of it for the first time) with a record of eccentric beliefs (primarily about divorce); he was heavily committed to his primary civil service duties, and his eyesight was rapidly deteriorating; but he was evidently a competent Latinist and he had recently produced some effectively controlled vernacular polemic. The more knowing council-member may well have wished that John Selden, for example, could have been persuaded to take Salmasius on. Like Salmasius, he already had a European reputation, and unlike Milton, he was an academic and a jurist. Cromwell is reputed to have tried to enlist Selden against *Eikon Basilike*,[3] but ideological issues aside, he was quite old, in failing health, and financially independent. The fact that the Council of State commissioned Milton seven or eight months after they first knew Salmasius was at work and weeks after Strickland had acted against the book in the United Provinces of the Netherlands suggests some hesitations.

The First Defense

Nor did Milton really proceed with much expedition. His response was approved for publication by the Council of State on 23 December 1650, and by late February 1651 it had appeared under the title *Joannis Miltoni Angli Pro Populo Anglicano Defensio Contra* Claudii Anonymi, *alias* Salmasii, *Defensionem Regiam* [*The Defense of John Milton, Englishman, on behalf of the English People against the Royal Defense of* Claudius the Nameless, *otherwise* Salmasius] (London, 1651). Nowadays, the work is usually called *Defensio Prima* or *First Defense*. Salmasius's book is substantial; Milton's response, more than 200 quarto pages, is about as long as *Eikonoklastes* and, like that work, is a point-by-point response, which necessarily allows his adversary to set the agenda for the debate. It has moments of great eloquence, and Milton's preface concludes with a sentiment that resonates even in translation with the heroism of England's republican experiment:

> Let us then approach this cause so righteous with hearts lifted up by a sure faith that on the other side stand deception, lies, ignorance and savagery, on our side light, truth, reason, and the hopes and teachings of all the great ages of mankind. (*CPW,* IV.i, 307)

But Salmasius's tract, while vituperative toward England's republican leaders, is a protracted essay on the constitutional implications of biblical, classical, and more recent history,[4] and Milton's own tract has about it much that may interest a historian of ideas but little that rewards a reader seeking the pleasure his vernacular prose can occasion. *Eikonoklastes* has the sustained aggression of a Cromwellian cavalry attack, ruthlessly and brilliantly outflanking the enemy; the *First Defense* is trench-warfare, ugly, attritional exchanges as each yard of ideological ground is contested; Ypres, not Dunbar. Yet stratagems and tactics can be teased from the inevitably dull reading that much of it now seems.

The Latin defenses function as a component of republican foreign policy. Salmasius's intention had been to render the republic a pariah state in Europe; Milton writes to limit that damage and to ease the normalization of England's international relations. Most pressingly, England's new government sought a closer relationship with the United Provinces of the Netherlands. The issues are quite complex. England had aided these Protestant inhabitants of what had been a Spanish province during their sixteenth-century wars of independence; indeed, such had been the political, cultural, and religious affinities between the nations that an act of union had been considered, and that concept would resurface in the mid–seventeenth century. However, England and the United Provinces were both seafaring, trading nations with incipient overseas empires; clashes of commercial and economic interest were inevitable. Internally, the constitutional affairs of the United Provinces were as fractured as England's had lately proved to be. The government was republican and federal; each province sent representatives to a grand council, the States General, which was usually dominated by the province of Holland. But the history of the United Provinces since the inception of the state had been dominated by the House of Orange, a quasi-royal dynasty that intermittently provided quasi-monarchical leadership through the hereditary office of stadtholder, or chief magistrate. The history of the United Provinces in the early modern period is often the history of conflict between the Orange stadtholder and the republican leadership. In 1650 the nation entered a phase that curiously parallelled events in England.

Stadtholder William II died (of natural causes), leaving as his heir the infant William III, too young to assume the office until 1672, which produced a vacuum in Dutch political leadership that the fiercely republican Johan de Witt was in the process of filling. The Orangists, though leaderless, were still a major component in the political land-scape of the United Provinces. The dynasty had been closely connected with the house of Stuart through the marriage of Mary, daughter of Charles I, to the late William II.

Positioning the new English republic to secure usefully friendly rela-tions with the United Provinces inevitably required an appreciation of the internal dynamics of Dutch politics. Dutch republicans confronted the Orangists, much as English republicans confronted the Stuarts. Mil-ton's Latin prose seconds a more traditional diplomatic approach. Four months after the publication of the *First Defense,* the English republic sent to the Hague a splendid ambassadorial delegation, which entered the city in a procession of 27 coaches and almost 250 retainers.[5] In any event, the mission proved unsuccessful, its impact largely sabotaged by Orangists and emigré English royalists. But preparation for it provides the pertinent immediate context for Milton's *First Defense.*

This delicate relationship is why we find Milton sustaining an account of constitutional history that emphasizes the instabilities of gov-ernmental systems and admits that in any state, monarchical rule may obtain at some points, republican rule at others:

> God himself bears witness to the right possessed by almost all peoples and nations of enjoying whatever form of government they wish, or of changing from one to another; this God asserts specifically of the Hebrews and does not deny of other nations. A republican form of gov-ernment, moreover, as being better adapted to our human circumstances than monarchy, seemed to God more advantageous for his chosen people; he set up a republic for them and granted their request for a monarchy only after long reluctance. To show that he had left to the people the choice of being governed by one man or by many, provided that this gov-ernment be just, God also established laws for the prospective king, if they should definitely desire one. (*CPW,* IV.i, 344)

Salmasius had forced the argument into a consideration of biblical precedent; Milton, though, is evidently thinking of contemporary Europe and of Dutch precedents for English actions. But where we may have expected a properly developed thesis in favor of republican govern-ment, we find instead the suggestion that republicanism is simply better suited to periods of greatest public morality, such as England and the United Provinces now enjoy:

> It is therefore a task for men of the utmost wisdom to discover what may be most suitable and advantageous for a people; certainly the same government is fitting neither for all peoples nor for one people at all times; now one form is better, now another, as the courage and industry of the citizens waxes or wanes. He who deprives a people of the power to choose whatever form of government they prefer surely deprives them of all that makes up civil liberty. (*CPW,* IV.i, 392)

The argument, although it has an ancient ancestry in Aristotelian political theory, functions as formal compliment to the Dutch people, currently showing the "courage and industry" to manage without the House of Orange. Of course, while a Dutch readership may be Milton's primary target, he has no interest in alienating other states that are monarchies. Hence, the disclaimer, "Whether the government of one man or several is in fact the better cannot be discussed here. Monarchy has indeed been praised by many famous men, provided that the sole ruler is the best of men and fully deserving of the crown; otherwise monarchy sinks most rapidly into the worst tyranny" (*CPW,* IV.i, 427). Again, he concludes, "I have completed the task which I had set for myself at the start, which was to defend at home and abroad the great works of my fellow citizens against the jealous rage and madness of this raving sophist, and to maintain the common rights of our people against the unrighteous tyranny of kings, doing so not because I hated kings, but only tyrants" (*CPW,* IV.i, 535). (We shall shortly see how this tune plays in his second Latin defense.)

But it is to the Dutch context he inevitably reverts, as he reproves Salmasius thus:

> Perhaps you may recall that the palmiest days of the Roman republic were after the expulsion of the kings? Could you forget the Dutch, whose republic, after they had driven out the Spanish king in long wars successfully waged, by glorious courage won her freedom? Now at her own expense the republic supports you as a knight of the blackboard, not, we hope, that the Dutch youths may from your lying sophistry learn to be so foolish as to choose a return to Spanish slavery rather than fall heir to the glorious freedom of their fathers! (*CPW,* IV.i, 429–30)

Of course, Salmasius is actually a beneficiary of Dutch Protestantism, taking his primary income from an academic post at Leyden. Milton needs to work on his Dutch readers to suggest that they are nurturing a viper in their bosoms, an ingrate whose pro-Stuart (and thus by implication pro-Orange) mercenary zeal threatens the great tradition of Dutch republicanism:

> We, you say, "attempt to justify our action by the example of the Dutch," and since, I suppose, you fear that the salary with which the Dutch support you, foul blight though you are, may be in danger should your slander of the English seem to cast a shadow on your Dutch patrons, you are eager to show how "unlike were the deeds of the two peoples." This comparison of yours is sheer falsehood in many respects, and the rest of it betrays the hand of a flatterer who fears he has not done enough for his dinner, but I shall say no more of it, for the English see no need for them to justify their own deeds by the example of any foreigners whatever. They have laws, and followed them; laws which they got from their fathers and which are here the most excellent, whatever may be the case in the rest of the world. They have as models their own forefathers, indomitable men, who never yielded to the unbridled sway of kings and who executed many of them when they made their rule unbearable. They were born in freedom, they live in independence, and they can make for themselves what laws they wish; they cherish particularly one law of great age, passed by Nature herself, which makes all laws, all rights, all civil government depend not on the desire of kings but primarily on the well-being of the better citizens. (*CPW,* IV.i, 533)

The exigencies of polemic may seem to betray Milton into a contradiction, for after struggling to show parallels between Dutch and English republicanism he now asserts that they are different. But the argument has more finesse than that. Simultaneously, he asserts three propositions. First, that Salmasius is a mercenary singing for his supper. Second, that the English people, whatever their admiration for the Dutch, are their own masters in pursuit of their own political destiny—a vital point in the context of the intended embassy, which was designed to impress the Dutch with an image of the wealth and power of the new republic. Finally, it suggests to a wide European readership that England has found remedies for England's problems; but that English republicans certainly are not in the business of exporting revolution. England has made its own choice; that is England's business, just as the choices of "the better citizens" of other nations are no business for England to involve itself in. As he remarks to Salmasius, "How the devil does it concern you what the English do amongst themselves?" (*CPW,* IV.i, 475).

The modern reader is inevitably drawn to the seamier side of the *First Defense*. Some aspects of the controversy exceed the usual bounds of political debate as we know it, although it is true that Salmasius had started the mudslinging in his vituperation against the English republic and its leaders. Milton seems to relish a new freedom in the neo-Latin medium, suggesting (as he had most certainly not done in *Eikonoklastes*) that Charles I had his hand down the occasional décolletage:

> Can you praise the purity and continence of one who is known to have joined the Duke of Buckingham in every act of infamy? There is no need to investigate his more private habits and hidden retreats when even in the theatre he kisses women wantonly, enfolds their waists and, to mention no more openly, plays with the breasts of maids and mothers. (*CPW,* IV.i, 408)

Buckingham was the favorite and first minister of James I and a widely unpopular figure by the time of his assassination; Milton is suggesting a misspent youth, and he does so with a sensationalism eschewed in vernacular tracts addressed to a domestic readership.

Salmasius posed a problem of a different kind: Milton had no academic reputation, yet he was engaging a scholar of international standing. In part he suggests that Salmasius is a mere mercenary, working as a hired gun for the Stuart dynasty rather than out of liberal conviction. We have seen something of that line already, and it does rather depend on not looking too closely at Milton's own government salary. More boldly, and perhaps more effectively, he chips away at Salmasius's scholarship, catching him out in his Latinity:

> You, the mighty critic, when hired at the king's expense to write the king's defence, not only failed to rouse the sympathy of any but fools with your most unnatural introduction which resembled nothing so much as the senseless wailing of women hired to mourn at funerals, but, furthermore, with your opening period you roused to laughter those who had hardly finished reading its manifold improprieties. What, I ask you, is "committing murder in the person of the king," what is "in the person of the king"? When was Latin ever spoken like that? (*CPW,* IV.i, 310)

Part of the duel that develops between Milton and the Continental apologists for kingship settles on such issues of Latinity: Who writes the better neo-Latin? Who comes closer to the model and ideal set by Cicero? Whose Latin is least corrupted by later Latin or by vernacular idioms?

Salmasius seems here to have come unstuck in his use of the word "persona," which in classical Latin meant, primarily, a "mask," and then a "dramatic character," and by extension a "person" but in the sense of the role one plays in the world rather than in the sense of an animate human body.[6] Milton portrays Salmasius as a kind of working man who sells the learning that a gentleman offers gratis for the causes he loves; in fact, Milton says, Salmasius is not really much better than a schoolteacher, a Holofernes priding himself in a pedantry that really betrays the shallowness of his culture:

> If I had time, or were it worth while, I might find in this single volume of yours so many barbarisms that, if you were punished according to your deserts, your little pupils would break all their sticks on your back. (*CPW*, IV.i, 488)

Personal abuse and academic rank-pulling remain a recurrent element in the Latin exchanges that follow.

The Second Defense

In May 1654 there appeared *Joannis Miltoni Angli Pro Populo Anglicano Defensio Secunda. Contra infamem libellum anonymum cui titulus, Regii sanguinis clamor ad coelum adversus parricidas Anglicanos* [*The Second Defense of John Milton, the Englishman, on behalf of the English People, against an infamous anonymous libel, of which the title is the Cry of the Royal Blood to the Sky against the English Parricides*]. This book is quite long, although shorter than the *First Defense*, and once more, as the title page makes clear, it is a response to a neo-Latin royalist attack. The "anonymous libel" in question, published in the Hague in 1652, produced something of a misprision on Milton's part. The editor of the Yale edition summarizes the issues:

> It is now beyond doubt that *Clamor* was the work of an Anglican priest Peter du Moulin, who was resident in England during the days of the Commonwealth and who was so little suspect that he was awarded a D. D. by Oxford in 1656. Du Moulin sent his manuscript to Salmasius in order that it might be published on the continent. Salmasius, in turn, transmitted it to Alexander More (Morus), a clergyman of the Reformed Church, who arranged for its printing by Adrian Vlacq at The Hague. In effect, More was a kind of editor-publisher of another man's book, but he involved himself more deeply by writing an abusive preface, which

appeared over the printer's name. More was associated with *Clamor* by many scholars on the continent, and Milton pounced upon him as the sole author. He was warned of his error by many friends, including Dury and Hartlib, but he persisted in his attribution of the work to More throughout *Defensio Secunda*. It may be said that, since *Clamor* was anonymous, Milton needed an author to suit the method of his argument, and that he accepted More as the most likely candidate.[7]

In fact, Adrian Vlacq actually wrote to Samuel Hartlib so that he could tip Milton off about the error of attributing authorship to the Scottish More, although the role of du Moulin, the son of a French Protestant divine, was not disclosed to Milton's camp.[8] (It shows something of the fascination this series of exchanges offered to a Continental readership that Vlacq, despite protestations of his royalism in the prefatory material to his edition of the *Clamor,* nevertheless sent Milton proof sheets of it in the hope of securing from him the copy for his response, and indeed Vlacq produced pirated reprints of the *Second Defense*.[9]) I can accept the argument that Milton needed an identifiable enemy, and as we shall see, More made a very easy target; yet ultimately it seems curiously inept of Milton to ignore information that inevitably would become known eventually to a wide European audience.

Milton conveys a new confident tone in the *Second Defense,* which reflects the military successes of the republic and the constitutional changes of 1653. Since February 1651, when the *First Defense* was published, all opposition to the new regime within the British Isles had been eliminated. In August 1651 at the Battle of Worcester, Charles II's army was utterly crushed. Republican England had also fought its first international war, the Anglo-Dutch war of 1652–1653, which ended in Dutch defeat and the death of their most illustrious admiral, van Tromp, leaving Cromwell to warn the Dutch, "The Lord has declared against you."[10] The pariah state emerged as "a principal player on the European stage, when diplomats were flocking to London, eager to recognize the newly confident government."[11] Constitutional uncertainties inherent in the rather improvised governmental structure of the Rump were pushed aside in April of 1653 by Cromwell's dismissal of that residue of the Long Parliament, and in the Instrument of Government, issued in December 1653, he was, as "Lord Protector," invested with powers analogous to those of the monarch who had been displaced. With the might of the New Model Army, functioning as a standing army, behind him, Cromwell was, unlike Charles I, perfectly able to fulfill that role without

effective opposition. With the Dutch obliged to seek terms, a new item
headed the republic's international agenda: improved relations with
Sweden.

All the confidence of the newly established Cromwellian ascendancy
is distilled into Milton's celebration of the Lord Protector and his government. This is a regime courted by other governments, among them
monarchies:

> Certainly other men in Parliament, and I myself in the Council, have
> often heard their [other states'] ambassadors and legates, when they were
> given an audience, so far from complaining about their grievances, actu-
> ally asking of their own free will for our friendship and alliance, even, in
> fact, congratulating us on our affairs in the names of their own kings and
> princes, wishing us well indeed and invoking eternal peace and security
> and the continuance of the same auspicious success. (*CPW,* IV.i, 652)

Cromwell is the state, and his powers and achievements transcend those
of mere monarchs:

> Commander first over himself, victor over himself, he had learned to
> achieve over himself the most effective triumph, and so, on the very first
> day that he took service against an external foe, he entered camp a vet-
> eran and past-master in all that concerned the soldier's life. . . .
>
> Cromwell, we are deserted! You alone remain. On you has fallen the
> whole burden of our affairs. On you alone they depend. In unison we
> acknowledge your unexcelled virtue. . . . Such have been your achieve-
> ments as the greatest and most illustrious citizen, the director of public
> counsels, the commander of the bravest armies, the father of your coun-
> try. It is thus that you are greeted by the spontaneous and heartfelt cries
> of all upright men. Your deeds recognize no other name as worthy of you;
> no other do they allow, and the haughty titles which seem so great in the
> opinion of the mob, they properly reject. For what is a title, except a cer-
> tain limited degree of dignity? Your deeds surpass all degrees, not only of
> admiration, but surely of titles too, and like the tops of pyramids, bury
> themselves in the sky, towering above the popular favor of titles. . . . By
> your deeds you have outstripped not only the achievements of our kings,
> but even the legends of our heroes. (*CPW,* IV.i, 668, 671–72)

Of course, Milton is saying, Cromwell *could* be king, but it would be
inappropriate, for that title sets a limit (albeit an exalted one) to his dignity and power. Cromwell does not rule as a tyrant, because tyranny is
what happens when a ruler has power over people who are at least as

good as himself; Cromwell, as the chief of men, rightly rules over others. The immediate occasion for this panegyric is the attack on Cromwell in the *Clamor*. But even when allowances are made for the exigencies of debate and perhaps for the rather overstated idiom of neo-Latin, Milton's praise of this *Übermensch* remains difficult to reconcile with the republican ethic.

Yet such rhetoric serves the moment well. It makes altogether more plausible that claim, articulated in the *First Defense* and repeated in the *Second*, that, "If I attack tyrants, what is this to kings, whom I am very far from classing as tyrants? As a good man differs from a bad, so much, I hold, does a king differ from a tyrant" (*CPW*, IV.i, 561). The argument meshes with the tract's sustained courtship of Queen Christina of Sweden. The English republic had always had good relations with Sweden and was currently engaged in active negotiation of a commercial agreement based on the Treaty of Uppsala signed between the countries in the month before the publication of the *Second Defense*. During the course of the English embassy to Sweden in 1653, it was learned that Queen Christina had looked at and apparently admired the *First Defense* (although, of course, she too may merely have been conducting herself diplomatically).[12] She also spoke to the English ambassador about Cromwell in terms that stressed his quasi-monarchical status:

> Much of the story of your General hath some parallel with that of my ancestor Gustavus the First, who, from a private gentleman of a noble family, was advanced to the title of Marshal of Sweden, because he had risen up and rescued his country from the bondage and oppression which the King of Denmark had put upon them, and expelled that king; and for his reward he was at last elected King of Sweden, and I believe that your General will be King of England in conclusion.[13]

Milton incorporates Christina's apparent goodwill toward the English republic in general and toward Cromwell and himself in particular into a purposeful panegyric that serves simultaneously to exculpate Milton from some of the strictures in the *Clamor* and further to distinguish English republicanism from a universal hostility to monarchical states:

> When I had fallen on such a time in my country's history as obliged me to become involved in a cause so difficult and so dangerous that I seemed to attack the whole right of kings, I found such a glorious, such a truly royal defender of my honesty to testify that I had uttered no word against kings, but only against tyrants—the pests and plagues of kings.

> How magnanimous you are, Augusta [i.e., Christina], how secure and well-fortified on all sides by a well-nigh divine virtue and wisdom. Not only could you read with so calm and serene a spirit, with such incredible objectivity and true composure of countenance a work that might seem to have been written against your own right and dignity, but you could adopt such a judgment against your own defender that you seem to most men even to award the palm to his opponent. With what honor, with what respect, O queen, ought I always to cherish you, whose exalted virtue and magnanimity are a source not alone of glory to you, but also of favor and benefit to me! They have freed me from all suspicion and ill-repute in the minds of other kings and by this glorious and immortal kindness have bound me to you for ever. . . . I should say that you are the daughter and only offspring of Adolphus, the unconquered and glorious king, did you not, Christina, as far outshine him as wisdom excels strength, and the arts of peace the crafts of war. (*CPW*, IV.i, 604–5)

Again, the decorum of neo-Latin discourse may require a greater fulsomeness than the vernacular. But certainly Milton is a chameleon republican, perfectly capable of praising the living monarch of another country to advance the diplomatic ends of the regime he serves. Milton as political writer is sometimes represented as a sort of innocent man of advanced integrity who has wandered into corrupt company. The guile of his *Second Defense* should surely preclude such wishful thinking.

Here and elsewhere Milton places a carefully crafted image of himself at the center of his response. This passage shows him a respecter of good monarchs whom good monarchs in turn respect. He gives us, too, extended narratives of his earlier life, necessarily so, because the *Clamor* had built a complex and destructive image of him as a lustful mercenary whose sins God punished with blindness. A narrative that has Milton "expelled from his college at Cambridge because of some disgrace, that he fled shame and his country and migrated to Italy"[14] requires a counternarrative in which Milton appears as heroic voice of Protestant freedom even in the very bastion of Catholicism:

> As I was on the point of returning to Rome, I was warned by merchants that they had learned through letters of plots laid against me by the English Jesuits, should I return to Rome, because of the freedom with which I had spoken about religion. For I had determined within myself that in those parts I would not indeed begin a conversation about religion, but if questioned about my faith would hide nothing, whatever the consequences. . . . What I was, if any man inquired, I concealed from no one. For almost two more months, in the very stronghold of the

> Pope, if anyone attacked the orthodox religion, I openly, as before, defended it. Thus, by the will of God, I returned again in safety to Florence. (*CPW,* IV.i, 619)

There is no other record of these events. But heroism is at the center of Milton's self-representation. His work with the pen mirrors the New Model Army's achievements with the sword: "For I did not avoid the toils and dangers of military service without rendering to my fellow citizens another kind of service that was much more useful and no less perilous" (*CPW,* IV.i, 552). As in *Eikonoklastes,* his engagement in polemic on behalf of the republic is represented as single combat, champion against champion: "When he [Salmasius] with insults was attacking us and our battle array, and our leaders looked first of all to me, I met him in single combat and plunged into his reviling throat this pen, the weapon of his own choice" (*CPW,* IV.i, 556). Probably the veterans of Naseby and Worcester could have advised him that a scrap in print is not quite the same as several pounds of chain-shot whistling past one's ears. But Milton has taken his honorable wounds in this fight:

> when the business of replying to the royal defense had been officially assigned to me, and at that same time I was afflicted at once by ill health and the virtual loss of my remaining eye, and the doctors were making learned predictions that if I should undertake this task, I would shortly lose both eyes, I was not in the least deterred by the warning. I seemed to hear, not the voice of the doctor (even that of Aesculapius, issuing from the shrine at Epidaurus), but the sound of a certain more divine monitor within. . . . I could at the cost of blindness alone fulfill the most honorable requirement of my duty. (*CPW,* IV.i, 587–88)

I doubt that reading and writing played any greater part than God's justice in the progress of his eye disease. Ours is an age without heroes, especially ones that proclaim their own heroism; yet we shall see in Milton's tracts of 1660, when to publish was to increase sharply the probabilities of a gory execution, that he too could stand alongside the martyrs of old in a final testament of faith.

This projection of a positive image of himself is complemented by Milton's savage attack on More. Here Milton is drawn to a widely circulated rumor that More's career had been interrupted by a sexual scandal involving a young woman in the household of Salmasius. By Milton's account, More had a record of promiscuity with servant women before the particular affair with "Pontia," and he used the opportunity of visiting Salmasius to discuss writing *Clamor* to seduce her and in the event to get her pregnant:

> He promised marriage. With this deluding hope, he ruined her. With this crime (I shrink from saying it, but it must be said) a minister of the holy gospel defiled even the house of his host. From the union resulted at length a marvellous and unnatural prodigy; not only the female but also the male conceived—Pontia a little More . . . ; and More conceived this empty wind-egg, from which burst forth the swollen Cry of the King's Blood. (*CPW*, IV.i, 569–70)

And so, for paragraph after paragraph, Milton plays on More's name, which means in Latin "mulberry bush" and in Greek "fool" or "knave." Perhaps, indeed, it passed for wit and was relished, although I confess it is a kind of humor that, for me, palled in the playground. Of course, Milton is answering a brutal abusiveness in kind; but a tract that swoops so wildly from name-calling and scandalmongering to lofty praise of Cromwellian magnanimity seems to me inherently unstable at the level of decorum. David Loewenstein, in the only considerable critical engagement with the Latin defenses in recent years, finds in this discursive riot a real strength and a major creative achievement:

> No other controversial pamphlet by Milton exploits such a variety of discursive modes and polemical postures to assert the power of the writer to operate creatively and forcefully in the social process. . . . In no other prose work of his controversial career does Milton modulate keys quite so skillfully and dramatically as he does in the *Second Defense*.[15]

Possibly a sympathetic contemporary reader, reared like Milton on the tradition of the academic disputation and genuinely convinced of the humor of his attacks and of the sincerity of his panegyrics—to Christina as well as Cromwell—could indeed relish it in all its diversity, and for Loewenstein that sense of Milton's controlling presence is enough of a unifying principle. For myself, I have never read the Latin defenses with pleasure.

The Third Defense

By the time Milton's third Latin defense was published, returns were emphatically diminishing. In October 1654 there appeared in the Hague *Alexandri Mori Ecclesiastae et Sacrarum Litterarum Professoris Fides*

Publica, Contra Calumnias Ioannis Miltoni [*The Public Faith of Alexander More, Preacher and Professor of Sacred Literature, against the Misrepresentations of John Milton*]; it was followed in spring 1655 with a supplementary publication, consisting chiefly of material documenting it, *Alexandri Mori Ecclesiastae et Sacrarum Litterarum Professoris Supplementum Fidei Publicae, Contra Calumnias Ioannis Miltoni* [*A Supplement to the Public Faith,* etc.]. *Fides Publica,* the first publication, develops three theses: that Milton is an absolutely depraved scoundrel, that Alexander More did not write the *Clamor,* and that More's personal biography is somewhat distorted in the *Second Defense.* The second thesis is by far the easiest to maintain. *Clamor*'s publisher, Vlacq, had tried to tell the English republicans about the mistaken authorship before the *Second Defense* was published, and indeed in a preface to *Fides Publica,* he could scarcely be plainer:

> Milton would have been more mindful of his own prudence, which he everywhere mentions so much, if he had made a serious inquiry as to who the author of that libel was, rather than assuming from a sinister suspicion or wrong information that Mr. More was its author and thundering so savagely against him when he is quite certain that he is not. . . . I . . . had written Hartlib two years before that Mr. More was not the author of the book titled *The Cry of the Royal Blood,* &c., and he replied to me on October 29, 1652, in these words, translated from English: "I am happy that you wrote to me that More is not the author of that vile and insulting libel." Now, is that man in his right mind who writes something other than that which he knows?[16]

Samuel Hartlib was not only a friend of Milton's but also, like Milton, an employee of the English republic in the area of foreign affairs; it would be surprising indeed if he had not shared with Milton the intelligence he had received. Indeed, Milton's case against More depended on intelligence gathering across much of the republican diplomatic community. But Milton evidently felt committed to a curious polemical strategy that rested so much on the vilification of a fairly insignificant individual who was not the prime mover behind the text Milton was attacking.

In August 1655 Milton issued in London his final Latin defense, Joannis Miltoni *Angli Pro Se Defensio contra* Alexandrum Morum, *Ecclesiasten, Libelli famosi, cui titulus,* Regii sanguinis clamor ad coelum adversus Parricidas Anglicanos, *authorem recte dictum* [*The Defense of Himself of John Milton the Englishman, against* Alexander More, *the Preacher, rightly said to*

be the author of a famous libel, of which the title is the Cry of the Royal Blood
to the Sky against the English Parricides]. Clearly Milton intends no
major shift in tactics, asserting on his title page that More was indeed
the author of the *Clamor*. The facts do need some massaging, however,
and Milton invests some effort in the argument that, because the *Clamor*
was published anonymously and because More was certainly involved in
that publication process, he can rightly be regarded as responsible for
it—in effect, he can be regarded as the author:

> I shall yield to you and grant this whole argument, that you are not the
> author of this libel titled *The Cry of the Royal Blood*. And yet, as perchance
> you now expect, you shall not escape thus. It is well known that this
> book is pieced together with certain proems and epilogues, an epistle to
> Charles and another to the reader, and that it is concluded with one
> poem, a thanksgiving for Salmasius, and another, a defamation of me. If I
> find that you wrote or contributed one page of this book, or even one
> versicle, if I find that you published it, or procured or persuaded anyone
> to publish it, or that you were in charge of its publication, or even lent
> yourself to the smallest part of the work, seeing that no one else comes
> forth, for me you alone will be the author of the whole work, the culprit
> and the crier. (*CPW,* IV.ii, 712–13)

This notion of accountability may have satisfied Milton; it may even
have satisfied some of his contemporary readership. Anyway, the hole he
had dug for himself becomes relatively easy to climb out of once he
engages with More's two publications in his own defense, thanks to
their other two principal theses (that Milton is a scoundrel and that
More has been misrepresented).

Indeed, in this tract, Milton's principal form of defense is almost
wholly attack. Milton revisits in far more detail the seamier side of
More's Continental career, the sex scandal associated with his departure
from Geneva, and the debauching of the maid of Salmasius's wife. How
curiously the argument has drifted, from the rights of free peoples to
determine their own form of government to whether a minor divine
copulated extramaritally with a serving girl in a summerhouse in a
country far from England:

> Return to Geneva where you were long ago found guilty of those crimes.
> Say only that you wish a legal judgment to be made concerning these
> matters for the sake of suppressing these calumnies; you will find those
> who, with the greatest good will, would share your wish to try these
> crimes by law, who would not refuse to post bail, nor to make a wager.

Witnesses will not be lacking. First shall come forth that gardener who saw you when you entered alone with the woman into that little garden cottage; he saw when that Claudia of yours closed the doors; he saw you afterwards come out openly embracing with the shameless woman, and so wanton that he thought he had seen the ancient obscene custodian of gardens, made not from a fig tree, as of old, but from a mulberry. (*CPW*, IV.ii, 756)

Indeed there is a joke here. The statues of the deity Priapus, which were placed in classical gardens as tutelary figures, were always represented with massive erections and were often made of fig wood; the gardener, seeing presumably the sexually aroused and presumably at least partially naked figure of More emerge from the summerhouse with the young woman, thinks he is seeing a different kind of priapic statue, this time one made from mulberry (because "Morus" means "mulberry"). Did the gardener really catch him thus aroused and compromised? I suppose it probably did matter for Milton's argument whether the charge was true. Indeed, the political eclipse of the prominent English regicide Henry Marten in the mid-1650s owed more than a little to sex scandals quite similar to More's, and such affairs have remained significant in public life well into the late twentieth century. Yet this tract never lives up to its opening declarations, that Milton is the last republican warrior still in arms for "the cause of liberty's defense" (*CPW*, IV.ii, 698); the war of Mr. More's gonads is a curiously bathetic coda to the struggle.

Chapter Seven

Church, State, and
the Good Old Cause

Civil Power and Hirelings

After the Restoration of King Charles II, to mark the twelfth anniversary of the execution of Charles I, the bodies of Oliver Cromwell, Oliver's son-in-law Henry Ireton, and John Bradshaw, the president of the regicide court, were taken from their tombs in Westminster Abbey and hanged in their shrouds from a gallows; thereafter their heads were impaled at Westminster Hall, alongside those of other regicides killed in the previous autumn, and their bodies were rolled into a pit under the gallows.[1] Readers may be rather surprised by the response of an early leader of the Quaker movement, George Fox, as he describes his recollection of witnessing the events:

> when the King came in they took [Cromwell] up & hanged him: & buryed him under Tyburn where he was rolled Into his grave with Infamy.
>
> And when I saw him hanginge there I saw his worde justly come upon him.
>
> But the Lords power & truth spreade: & wee was promised still liberty & when it was going forward one or other dirty spirits put in papers & set stop to it that seemed to be for us.
>
> And there was about 700 friends in prison upon contempts to O. Cromwell, and Richard & their government when the king came in: he set them all at liberty.[2]

By the time Fox wrote this, however, Charles II had set most of them back in prison. Fox may not have been wholly guileless; possibly he emphasized his own dislike of Cromwell to secure a modus vivendi with the restored Stuart establishment (a rather ambitious program, if that indeed was his objective).[3]

The word that Cromwell had broken was his promise after his miraculous victory at the Battle of Dunbar to amend religion in England as part of a program of radical reform. Central to any such reform would have been the abolition of compulsory local church taxes, known as tithes, which were contrived to fund a state church without resort to state funds. The system was ancient and found its justification in the provision to be made for the priesthood in Old Testament times. Its advantages in the early modern period lay in the possibilities of making such provision without raising revenue through national fiscal measures, though the practice had grave practical disadvantages. Livings in towns, for example, were notoriously underfunded. However, tithes required the payment of local taxes to support a minister whom radical parishioners may well have regarded as remote from their faith. Woolrych summarizes the arguments thus:

> There were at least five grounds for objecting to tithes, variously maintained by different classes of opponent, and ranging from the purely doctrinal to the purely economic. Of the first kind the commonest was that they were popish and superstitious, the argument being that they had lost their divine sanction when the Law gave place to the Gospel and the Levitical priesthood to an apostolic ministry. Strict separatists opposed them even more strongly because tithes maintained a parochial clergy whose doctrine and ordinances they rejected and a national established church whose very existence offended their consciences. As much as a third of the tithes paid in England, however, went not to parish incumbents but to lay impropriators who at some time since the Reformation had acquired the rectorial tithes formerly appropriated by religious houses. This was obviously a grievance in itself, and it was one of several causes of a further one, namely that maintenance by tithes resulted in gross and irrational inequalities in the value of parish livings. Finally, and most basic, tithes were a severe but very unequal economic burden, falling most heavily on smaller landholders, who still generally paid them in kind.[4]

The issue had been hotly debated, especially during the period of the nominated "Barebones Parliament" of 1653, at a time when a radical, godly revolution within church and state had seemed possible. Episcopalians and Presbyterians, of course, wished for the retention of tithes, and so too did some Independent Congregationalists, who took an essentially reformist position, recognizing the faults of the current system but insisting that some form of church tax was necessary for the proper promulgation of the gospel within a Christian commonwealth. Sectaries like the Quaker Fox utterly abhorred the system, which in their view incorporated church and state into a repressive alliance against them. But other radicals were less stable and less predictable in their view, and Levelers, for a while, entertained the reformist middle way.[5]

The group Milton was most closely associated with politically, the emerging figures of the Cromwellian ascendancy, probably inclined to reformism. In some respects, however, Milton nursed a deeper radicalism than the men he worked with. Like Fox in the early 1650s, Milton had expected Cromwell to secure the abolition of tithes and take the associated step of finally separating church and state to the exclusion of the magistrate from religious matters. Thus his sonnet, "To the Lord General Cromwell," which he dated May 1652, explicitly connects the providential victories of the second Civil War with a radical agenda he urged Cromwell to follow:

> Cromwell, our chief of men, who through a cloud
>   Not of war only, but detractions rude,
>   Guided by faith and matchless fortitude
>   To peace and truth thy glorious way hast ploughed,
> And on the neck of crowned fortune proud
>   Hast reared God's trophies and his work pursued,
>   While Darwen stream with blood of Scots imbrued,
>   And Dunbar field resounds thy praises loud,
> And Worcester's laureate wreath; yet much remains
>   To conquer still; peace hath her victories
>   No less renowned than war, new foes arise
> Threatening to bind our souls with secular chains:
>   Help us to save free conscience from the paw
>   Of hireling wolves whose gospel is their maw.[6]

Milton did not contribute pamphlets to the heated debates of the early 1650s about tithes and the related issue of the exclusion of the magistrate from matters of conscience. We do not know why, because plainly these matters concerned him greatly. Perhaps the many tasks placed on him in defense of the republic precluded addressing the subject at length; perhaps his status as a civil servant dissuaded him from public controversy with his political masters; perhaps he felt that, because he was for once a political insider, he could exert his influence more personally and directly. However, in 1659, after the death of Oliver Cromwell, he published two pamphlets on the interconnected issues of the separation of civil powers from ecclesiastic matters and on the abolition of tithes, *A Treatise of Civil power in Ecclesiastical causes: shewing That it is not lawfull for any power on earth to compell in matters of Religion* (February 1659) and *Considerations Touching The likeliest means to remove Hirelings out of the church. Wherein is also discourc'd Of* Tithes, Church-fees, Church-revenues; *And whether any maintenance of ministers can be settl'd by law* (August 1659).

Milton is entering, rather belatedly, into a mature debate revived in the Indian summer of the English republic. Early in his own career as public servant, he had sent to Sir Henry Vane, a radical grandee clearly to the left of Cromwell, a sonnet urging him to press on with the campaign to separate church and state and defining as central to good government a proper understanding of these issues:

> to know
> Both spiritual power and civil, what each means,
> What severs each, thou hast learned, which few have done.
> The bounds of either sword to thee we owe.[7]

In 1659, Vane had emerged once more as a significant figure from whom Milton could have expected a purposeful leadership, and the tithes debate was reanimated—although more faintly than in the days of the Rump or the early days of the Protectorate—as part of radical republicanism's final gesturing.[8] Milton woke up to his last opportunity to speak for himself in prose, and for the first time since 1645, he writes as an individual contributor to a controversy, not as a team player obliged to do what the circumstances required of him in defense of his party or faction. As he put it in the epistle "To the Parlament of the Commonwealth of England with the Dominions Therof," which prefaces *Civil Power* (the Parliament is Richard Cromwell's, which had assembled shortly before publication):

> *Of civil libertie I have written heretofore by the appointment, and not without the approbation of civil power: of Christian liberty I write now; which others long since having don with all freedom under heathen emperors, I should do wrong to suspect, that I now shall with less under Christian governors, and such especially as profess openly thir defence of Christian libertie; although I write this not otherwise appointed or induc'd then by an inward perswasion of the Christian dutie which I may usefully discharge herin to the common Lord and Master of us all.* (*CPW,* VII, 240)

In part, the epistle serves as a *captatio benevolentiae,* assuring a new assembly of Milton's long record as public servant and of his loyalty to a system of government that that new assembly now represents. But in the differentiation of the tract that follows from the tracts he had written at the government's instruction in defense of the realm, the epistle defines a new beginning in his practices as prose writer.

The two tracts of 1659 are very similar in style, in their mode of exposition, and in the way Milton presents himself to his readers. These are in some ways among his plainest tracts. There are few similes or metaphors; the language is sober and purposeful, almost without word-play.[9] Milton weaves into his text close references to scripture, involving his own prose with proof texts, borrowing words and phrases from cited material into his exposition, and operating with a studied proximity to the scriptural evidence that substantiates his argument. Consider the following passage from *Civil Power,* which is wholly typical of both tracts:

> For he [God] hath not only given us this gift [of freedom from the laws and ceremonies required under the Old Testament] as a special privilege and excellence of the free gospel above the servile law, but strictly also hath commanded us to keep it and enjoy it. *Gal.* 5. 13. *you are calld to libertie.* 1 *Cor.* 7. 23. *be not made the servants of men. Gal.* 5. 14. *stand fast therfore in the libertie wherwith Christ hath made us free; and be not intangl'd again with the yoke of bondage.* Neither is this a meer command, but for the most part in these forecited places accompanied with the verie waightiest and inmost reasons of Christian religion. *Rom.* 14. 9, 10. *for to this end Christ both dy'd and rose and reviv'd, that he might be Lord both of the dead and living. But why dost thou judge thy brother? &c.* how presum'st thou to be his lord, to be whose only Lord, at least in these things, Christ both dy'd and rose and livd again? *We shall all stand before the judgment seat of Christ.* why then dost thou not only judge, but persecute in these things for which we are to be accountable to the tribunal of Christ only, our Lord and lawgiver? (*CPW,* VII, 263–64)

Milton in *Tetrachordon* had written in exegetical mode, teasing the meaning from the biblical texts chosen for explication. But here the idiom is rather different. The words of the scripture permeate his language, setting the horizon to his argument. Note how the vocabulary from the proof text becomes the vocabulary for Milton's own prose. Paradoxically the effect is both unspectacular and very striking. Milton is locking his imagination and his eloquence within the constraints of the biblical idiom in a way that manifests a new humility to the revealed word of God.

But both these tracts are curiously introverted, focusing not outward on the politics of tolerationism and tithe-abolition, but inward on the promptings of the spirit and on the scriptures. As Woolrych, with an understandable impatience, puts it, "The English Revolution generated many more exciting controversies than that over tithes, but few so voluminous."[10] Although both tracts explicitly address Parliament, neither engages in systematic fashion earlier discussions of the subject, despite the welter of possible pro-tithe pamphlets he could have taken as his starting point. Perhaps such a change in polemical idiom reflects, among other things, the introversion and the disabilities of Milton's now absolute blindness; these are works that brood over the one text that is uniquely privileged in the Christian tradition, the Bible, and relegate all others from consideration.

But, again paradoxically, while the tracts do not seek out engagement with other controversialists, they are explicitly and efficiently targeted at an intended readership. These tracts are briefings for busy people, writings characterized by a display of austere brevity. Thus, *Civil Power* concludes,

> Pomp and ostentation of reading is admir'd among the vulgar: but doubtless in matters of religion he is learnedest who is planest. The brevitie I use, not exceeding a small manual, will not therfore, I suppose, be thought the less considerable, unless with them perhaps who think that great books only can determin great matters. I rather chose the common rule, not to make much ado where less may serve. Which in controversies and those especially of religion, would make them less tedious, and by consequence read ofter, by many more, and with more benefit. (*CPW*, VII, 272)

Hirelings ends with a similar declaration of stark functionalism, one that challenges his readers to take or to leave (at their peril) the advice Milton offers:

> Thus much I had to say; and, I suppose, what may be anough to them who are not avariciously bent otherwise, touching the likeliest means to remove hirelings out of the church; then which nothing can more conduce to truth, to peace and all happines both in church and state. If I be not heard nor beleevd, the event will bear me witnes to have spoken truth: and I in the mean while have borne my witnes not out of season to the church and to my countrey. (*CPW*, VII, 320–21)

Since his earliest antiprelatical tracts, Milton had developed a symbolic universe in which the purity of truth and godly religion exhibited itself in its unadorned simplicity while corruption of religion found expression in accretion, in the unnecessary adornment of ceremony and vestments, in the redundant supplementation of the patristic tradition, in the superimpositions of Catholic practice on the truth of the gospel. In both *Civil Power* and *Hirelings,* that symbolic dichotomy produces a polemical minimalism of lean eloquence.

Another long-standing Miltonic concern, his hatred of professional clergymen, reaches its most extreme expression. As Woolrych rightly remarks, "Here is as harsh a strain of anticlericalism as anywhere in his works, and it is directed now not just against prelates or Presbyterians but against the whole body of the beneficed clergy."[11] In Milton's antiprelatical pamphlets, the bishops and episcopalian clergy are represented as obscene ingestion-machines, mawing down the material resources of the church as they would a mighty feast. In the tracts that follow the first edition of *The Doctrine and Discipline of Divorce,* Presbyterian divines are depicted as ravenous wolves, roaming from living to living to gorge themselves on the carrion remains of episcopacy. Now even the beneficed Congregational Independents are condemned for their material concerns with income and prosperity and status, which prompt their demand that they be kept by the tithes paid by those they should serve gratis:

> these, from whom there is no sanctuarie, seise out of mens grounds, out of mens houses thir other goods of double, somtimes of treble value, for that, which did not covetousnes and rapine blinde them, they know to be not thir own by the gospel which they preach. (*Hirelings, CPW,* VII, 296)

Possibly more knowing clergymen may have reflected that it was somewhat easier to take a lofty view if, like Milton, one had a state salary approaching £300 per annum.

But there is a real note of religious radicalism in Milton's arguments and the values they are premised on. What he is advocating is a very different kind of ministry. It may be pursued by modestly educated but godly people who have the spirit within them: "They who after him [Christ] first taught it [the gospel], were . . . unlearned men: they who before *Hus* and *Luther* first reformd it, were for the meanenes of thir condition calld, *the poore men of Lions*" (*CPW,* VII, 302).[12] He writes warmly and at some length in praise of itinerant preachers, going out, in the

footsteps of the apostles, to spread the gospel where it has least penetrated, and he writes, too, in praise of the informality of such missions:

> For notwithstanding the gaudy superstition of som devoted still igno-
> rantly to temples, we may be well assur'd that he who disdaind not to be
> laid in a manger, disdains not to be preachd in a barn; and that by such
> meetings as these, being, indeed, most apostolical and primitive, they
> will in a short time advance more in Christian knowledge and reforma-
> tion of life, then by the many years preaching of such an incumbent, I
> may say, such an incubus oft times, as will be meanly hir'd to abide long
> in those places. (*CPW*, VII, 304–5)

That rare example of wordplay (on "incumbent" and "incubus") stands
out boldly in the stark plainness of his late prose, almost as a recollection
of his earliest vehemence. Ideologically, the passage is fascinating,
almost tantalizing. By the late 1650s, the group most associated with
itinerant preaching *and* informality of meeting place *and* an unlearned
and unbeneficed ministry was most certainly the Quakers. We know
that after the Restoration, Milton counted some prominent Quakers,
such as Thomas Ellwood, among his circle of friends; we know, too, that
when he fled plague-stricken London in 1665, he went to Chalfont St.
Giles, a center of Quaker activity; and lately, several critics have identified Quaker-like elements in his late poetry.[13] I am not suggesting that
Milton in 1659 *was* a Quaker. But to an attentive contemporary reader,
he is unmistakably showing his approval for a style of ministry that
closely resembles the evangelical practices of early Quakers, and it may
usefully be observed that tithe reform was eagerly if unsuccessfully promoted through 1659 with a spectacular level of petitioning by Quaker
groups.[14]

The End of the Republic

Yet anti-tithe activism constituted a late flourish of midcentury radicalism. The long winter of the royalist counterrevolution, largely unno-
ticed, drew on apace. The complex events of 1659–1660 require some
account if we are to make much of Milton's final republican writings.

After the death of Cromwell, his son Richard had acceded to the title
and role of Lord Protector and had called a parliament. Lacking Oliver's
closeness to the senior officers of the New Model Army, the real guaran-
tors of republicanism, Richard failed to meet such army expectations as
the payment of back salary, and his regime ended in a muted military

coup. This coup was followed by the reassembly of the purged remnant, the Rump, of the Long Parliament that had first met in 1640, now just 42 strong. Civilian and military republicans could well have saved the regime had both wings cooperated and had there been greater unanimity both within Parliament and within the army. However, in the elation following the successful suppression of a quite serious royalist uprising ("Booth's Rebellion"), relationships so deteriorated that Parliament attempted to remove certain prominent officers, and those officers in turn surrounded Parliament and forced its dispersal, establishing a "Committee of Safety"—in effect, a new government. However, the commander of those regiments of the New Model Army controlling Scotland, General George Monck, following a course of action whose motivation is as obscure today as it was to his contemporaries, refused to recognize this development. He marched on London, the forces of his opponents melted away, and he recalled the Long Parliament, including those members excluded in the winter of 1648 by Pride's Purge. He required it to establish new elections without disablement of Presbyterian-royalists and thereafter to end its rule. The new Parliament, much as was expected, was dominated by elements sympathetic to restoring Charles II to his father's throne, and by spring 1660 the game was over.[15]

Milton's two tracts of 1659 already reflect an awareness of the increasing instability in government. Whereas *Civil Power* is addressed to Richard Cromwell's parliament, *Hirelings* has an epistle to the restored Rump. Both tracts take a relatively extreme line on the relationship of church and state, one that aligned Milton with the more militant groups of the late 1650s. But the second tract does, in its conclusion, disclose a certain edginess about whether it will find a hearing in current circumstances ("*If I be not* heard nor beleeved"—quoted above; my emphasis). Hill most shrewdly observes that "Milton's principal concern henceforth was to reunite the radicals, to bring an end to their self-righteous divisions. . . . For now the survival of the Revolution itself was at stake."[16]

Milton's last works consist of three publications—the two editions of *The Readie and Easie Way to Establish a Free Commonwealth* (February and April 1660) and *Brief Notes Upon a late Sermon* (April 1660)—and three slighter and rather problematic documents—*A Letter to a Friend* (probably October 1659), *Proposalls of Certaine Expedients* (late 1659), and *The Present Means, and Brief Delineation of a Free Commonwealth* (spring 1660)—all of which remained in manuscript in Milton's lifetime. I have demonstrated elsewhere[17] how each publication is fine-tuned to meet the dynamic political context in which Milton sought to operate, and I have argued that, in some senses, the changes generally came too quickly for him to be wholly successful in that endeavour. I shall not reiterate those arguments here. Instead, my critical focus is on the extraordinary vividness with which, in his most considered statement on the impending counterrevolution, the second edition of *The Readie and Easie Way*, he defines two contrasting visions, one of the squalid horror of restored monarchy, the other of a stable, rational republic, wholly committed to safeguarding both the rights of property and of intellectual and religious freedom. No other English regime has had so eloquent and so poignant a memorial.

A republic is governed by men acknowledged to be as mortal, as undivine, as the electorate that selects them. They live as ordinary people live. Their material requirements are not exorbitant. They surround themselves with no court ritual. They may be addressed, civilly but without adoration, much as those who select them address each other. But in a monarchy in the early modern period, there is an assumption that the King is more than a mere mortal; rather, his rule is deemed to be divinely sanctioned, he is God's anointed representative, and he is separated from ordinary people by an aura of the divine. Social intercourse with the King is circumscribed by and mediated through a complex set of rituals premised on his special status. His material requirements far outstrip those of ordinary people. The ideologies of republicanism and royalism, however, are further distinguished by their proximity to or distance from an external reality. In a republic, the rulers behave as ordinary people, distinguished perhaps by their wisdom and experience, because that is what they are. In a monarchy, even though the King may claim a semidivine status, in reality he is a person of ordinary abilities, and the mystique conceals (though not from Milton) the greed, indulgence, and dissipation of the royal lifestyle. Thus, Milton writes,

> [in a free commonwealth] they who are greatest, are perpetual servants and drudges to the public at thir own cost and charges, neglect thir own affairs; yet are not elevated above thir brethren; live soberly in thir families, walk the streets as other men, may be spoken to freely, familiarly, friendly, without adoration. Wheras a king must be ador'd like a Demigod, with a dissolute and haughtie court about him, of vast expence and luxurie, masks and revels, to the debaushing of our prime gentry both male and female; not in thir passetimes only, but in earnest, by the loos imploiments of court service, which will be then thought honorable. There will be a queen also of no less charge; in most likelihood out-

landish and a Papist; besides a queen mother such alreadie; together with both thir courts and numerous train: then a royal issue, and ere long several'ly thir sumptuous courts; to the multiplying of a servile crew, not of servants only, but of nobility and gentry, bred up then to the hopes not of public, but of court offices; to be stewards, chamberlains, ushers, grooms, even of the close-stool; and the lower thir mindes debas'd with court opinions, contrarie to all vertue and reformation, the haughtier will be thir pride and profuseness. . . . As to the burden of expence, to our cost we shall soon know it; for any good to us, deserving to be termd no better then the vast and lavish price of our subjection and their debausherie; which we are now so greedily cheapning, and would so fain be paying most inconsideratly to a single person; who for any thing wherin the public really needs him, will have little els to do, but to bestow the eating and drinking of excessive dainties, to set a pompous face upon the super-ficial actings of State, to pageant himself up and down in progress among the perpetual bowings and cringings of an abject people, on either side deifying and adoring him for nothing don that can deserve it. For what can hee more then another man? (*CPW,* VII, 425–26)

Even now, of course, the British royal family does indeed have its several courts, for the Prince of Wales and for the Queen Mother as well as for the Queen herself; and royal processions, perhaps such as those associated with great state occasions like the royal weddings of the 1980s, give to a television audience both in the United Kingdom and abroad some sense of what a royal pageant may have been like in the early modern period.

But the court of Charles I is distinguished within the long history of the British monarchy by its extraordinary elaborations of court ritual, as Sharpe has recently so evocatively demonstrated. Indeed the 1630s had borne witness to a proliferation of courts, for Henrietta Maria and Charles Prince of Wales as well as the King. A new sanctity clothed the private quarters of the King, and, apart from princes of the blood, as Sharpe explains, "Charles ordered that none have access to the bed-chamber but the gentlemen of that chamber and those, such as doctors or barbers, who necessarily attended the king on particular occasions." Those gentlemen who performed intimate duties for the King were often of high birth, at least upper gentry class. For example, the poet Thomas Carew, himself a knight's son, was Charles's "sewer in ordi-nary," with a regular responsibility for supervising the setting of the King's dinner table and the serving of food. The conduct of such ser-vants was as ceremonial as Laudian church ritual. The King's carver would enter the presence chamber in the company of a gentleman usher and make three bows to the several parts of the room before approaching the table. The gentleman usher who gave the King a towel to dry himself after washing before dinner was to carry it out of the room raised above his head as if it were a sacred object. When the King went to church, his donation was to be handed by a gentleman usher to the most eminent nobleman present, who was then to kiss it before giving it to the King, who would then offer it to the officiating clergyman.[18] And so it went.

As Sharpe notes, "Such rituals publicly emphasied the reverence due to the king's body and the mystical majesty of monarchy."[19] Milton understood that game well enough, and his account builds a careful crescendo, "stewards, chamberlains, ushers, grooms, even of the close-stool," that culminates in the final reminder of the ordinariness of the King; he, too, defecates (*CPW,* VII, 425). The "groom of the close-stool" was indeed a court office in the early modern period,[20] and that intimate body servant, from the same social echelon as these other servants, did indeed accompany and assist the King when he used his close-stool (a sort of precursor of the commode). All that ritual and that pomp and hierarchy, designed to separate the King from common humankind, ends contradictorily in confirming that the same biological imperatives drive kings as other people. Like Swift's Celia, the King, evidently, shits. A monarchy shamefully causes people to contend for the job of attending the King in this bodily function rather than for the honorable offices that would be open to them in a republic.

But the passage rehearses a richer array of republican values. The court wastes money as well as talent, and it does so in the pursuit of immoral entertainment. Both elements are central to its defining cultural forms, "masks and revels." Milton himself had written a court masque, *Comus,* albeit one performed in the provincial court of the President of the Council of Wales and the Marches, and that was a long time ago. Now, in 1660, he invokes a recollection of that court excess and depravity for criticism of which William Prynne, once a leading parliamentarian, now an advocate of restoration, had lost his ears in the early years of opposition to Charles I. As Hill observes, Milton is looking to reconstruct a wide spectrum of support. Masques were indeed singularly expensive entertainments, possible only in a context of conspicuous extravagance, and they were ephemeral events performed before a closed and privileged audience. Sharpe notes that the five-year average cost of masques in the mid-1630s was only £1,310 per annum—a figure that "cannot be said to loom large" in the larger annual expenditure of the crown of £636,536,[21] but it would have taken an agricultural laborer working a six-day week about 175 years to earn that much, and it constituted a very considerable sum to Puritans who thought such entertainment sinful. Within that total expenditure of the crown, the largest items were pensions (that is, payments to dependents of all sorts) and the maintenance of the royal households of the King, Queen, and princes ("over £135,000, not including wardrobe expenses of more that £26,000"). Shopping would seem to have been something of a royal preoccupation.

Although we must not too eagerly snatch at stereotypes, Puritans did, characteristically, represent themselves as following an austere lifestyle and avoiding such spectacular indulgence. Cromwell's plain attire was frequently remarked upon, for example:

> In August 1652 the Venetian Ambassador commented on "his unpretending manner of life, remote from all display and pomp, so different from the former fashion of this kingdom." Men noticed the "plain black clothes, with grey worsted stockings" which Oliver wore when he dissolved the rump. Even when he was Lord Protector a Quaker . . . commented on his rough coat, "not worth three shillings a yard," and his court was so far from ostentation that royalist propagandists preferred to concentrate on Mrs Cromwell's meanness.[22]

Cromwell retained a distinct accessibility. George Fox, whose comments on Cromwell's gibbeting began this chapter, met him in Hyde Park and was invited home to continue the earnest conversation he had begun.[23] Hermann Mylius, a German diplomatic in London, noted in his diary that he had met Cromwell walking with Mrs. Cromwell in St. James's Park; though they had never met before, "I greeted him in proper manner, and he politely enough saluted me back."[24] The privateness of the Caroline privy chambers, secreting the King from his subjects like the holiest of holies, contrasts sharply with a government style defined by Cromwell. Although Milton, addressing a post–Protectorate readership, is careful to make little of Cromwell, a Cromwellian aesthetic informs much of his observations on the virtues of republicanism.

Milton also celebrates the republic as an English national institution and as a bulwark against Catholicism. Caroline court life was a local variation on the international culture of absolutism, best manifest in the Catholic courts of Bourbons and Hapsburgs. The republic, although analogous to that of the Protestant United Provinces in particular, is an English experiment. It was founded on "the blood of so many thousand faithfull and valiant *English* men" (*CPW,* VII, 423–24). If it collapses, the English people must endure "the common laughter of *Europ*" (*CPW,* VII, 423). A restored Stuart court, in contrast, would be a bastion of popery and the resort of aliens. The Queen Mother, Henrietta Maria, is "outlandish and a Papist," and in all probability Charles II will marry someone who is also a foreign Catholic (*CPW,* VII, 425). But then the Stuarts always were soft on Catholicism and prodigal of the English national interest. Charles I had connived at the massacre of Protestant settlers by the native Catholics of Ireland, and he had plotted to bring an Irish Catholic army into England to fight on his side in the first Civil War (*CPW,* VII, 410). The republic had secured for England "all *Scotland* as to our conquest . . . which never any of our kings could conquer" (*CPW,* VII, 424). This association of republicanism with English national interest relies on a strategy Milton first used in the tracts of 1649.

Milton tries to situate all his Puritan readers from throughout that broad ideological spectrum as if at a crossroads that offers the easy road to security by way of republicanism and the hard and uncertain route of royalist restoration, leading to unpredictable dangers even for turncoats. He asks those readers to ponder what they know about the die-hard royalists, the men who had gone with the young King into exile and who are now to return. Various changes of government in 1659–1660 had eroded some of the apparatuses of press control, and royalist propaganda, often in the form of scurrilous lampoons and broadsides, had been widely disseminated with increasing boldness, especially since the turn of the year.[25] Consider, Milton urges, the values implicit in that torrent of abuse:

> Let them but now read the diabolical forerunning libells, the faces, the gestures that now appeer foremost and briskest in all public places; as the harbingers of those that are in expectation to raign over us; let them but hear the insolencies, the menaces, the insultings of our newly animated common enemies crept lately out of thir holes, thir hell, I maight say, by the language of thir infernal pamphlets, the spue of every drunkard, every ribald. . . . Let our zealous backsliders forethink now with themselves, how thir necks yok'd with these tigers of Bacchus, these new fanatics of not the preaching but the sweating-tub, inspir'd with nothing holier then the Venereal pox, can draw one way under monarchie. (*CPW,* VII, 452–53)

Former readers of Milton may perhaps have recalled his comments in *Eikonoklastes* on the swaggerers that sought to arrest the five members, "the ragged Infantrie of Stewes and Brothels; the spawn and shiprack of Taverns and Dicing Houses" (*CPW*, III, 380–81). To return the King is to return this ghastly army and the debauched culture associated with them. The voice Milton would have his readers hear comes, not from the sectaries' improvised pulpits of the preaching tub, but from the sweating tub, from the medical apparatus for treating venereal disease in which the patient sat on a stool in a large tub while his privates were bathed in the supposedly healing smoke of the material smouldering in a small fire underneath him; not an obvious source of balanced and constructive comment. Pox and drunkard's vomit characterize this band, and yet sober Puritans currently were prepared to turn their coats and invite them into power. But what then? What would be the fate, say, of those Presbyterians who started the war with the King in 1642? What kind of understanding could they expect once the New Model Army has been disbanded, probably without back pay, and the only standing army is one made up of "the fiercest Cavaliers . . . and perhaps again under *Rupert*" (*CPW*, VII, 454)? And what can the soldiers of the New Model Army expect under such circumstances? Surely, at the least "they may . . . be questiond for being in arms against thir king," just as anyone who has lent money to the republic "must then take thir turn to be made delinquents" (*CPW*, VII, 454).

Restoration, then, emerges in Milton's account as a crazy leap in the dark, risking prosecution, inviting into power aliens and Catholics, empowering the savage Cavaliers expelled in the civil wars, and abandoning the independency of religious conscience that most Puritans had enjoyed in the 1650s. In contrast, Milton offers a constitutional settlement of a kind that could only have been underwritten by the leaders of the army in that it in no way depends on a popular mandate. Rather, it is a solution that keeps power within the ranks of those who guarantee not to invite back the Stuarts and who accept the notion of the freedom of conscience. Milton's model for the state postulates a permanent assembly of such godly folk, elected for their lifetimes by those enfranchised not only by property but also by their acceptance of the central tenets of republican tolerationism. This standing assembly, moreover, has relatively little power, because much of that is to be devolved to permanent regional assemblies, which would be, like Parliament, standing committees of the propertied and godly. These assemblies would underwrite law and order in their regions while actively promoting an education-led cultural revolution to build a new kind of godly citizen, realizing in part the agenda of *Of Education*:

> They should have heer also schools and academies at thir own choice, wherin thir children may be bred up in thir own sight to all learning and noble education. . . . This would soon spread much more knowledge and civilitie, yea religion through all parts of the land, by communicating the natural heat of government and culture more distributively to all extreme parts, which now lie numm and neglected, would soon make the whole nation more industrious, more ingenuous at home, more potent, more honorable abroad. (*CPW,* VII, 460)

For a moment Milton makes the vision of a godly commonwealth of city states, each a center of learning and civic responsibility, seem attainable. Within weeks, his dream was a poignant waymark on a road not taken.

Alongside the utopian vision, Milton projected another scenario, more vividly realized, of a returning chaos invested in the populace's vulgar royalism to be expressed in mob violence on the godly. He expresses a blind man's fear of the "noise and shouting of a rude multitude" (*CPW,* VII, 442), the sort of crowds that turned up for the hanging, drawing, and quartering of Milton's former associates later that year, roaring as the executioners exhibited their victims' heads and hearts with what Pepys termed "great shouts of joy."[26] In the spring of 1660, Milton knew the cost of defeat was high, and he can have entertained little expectation that he, who had defended the regicide before Europe, would escape that sickening ride to the gallows, that throttling, and that evisceration by the executioner's knife. No wonder in those months of helter-skelter advance to the restoration he had yearned to put a halt to instability; no wonder the tract is haunted by fears of "commotions, changes, novelties and uncertainties" (*CPW,* VII, 434). Yet in that giddy world, Milton still stands up for "that which is not call'd amiss *the good Old Cause*" (*CPW,* VII, 462). Unlike most of the old revolutionaries, Milton indeed goes down fighting.

Chapter Eight

Miscellaneous and Posthumous Publications

Of True Religion

Milton wrote only one more work of controversial prose, *Of True Religion, Hæresie, Schism, Toleration, And what best means may be us'd against the growth of Popery,* "written and published sometime between March 13 and May 6, 1673."[1] The years since the Restoration had witnessed the major triumph of his literary career, the publication of *Paradise Lost* (1667), and the utter eclipse of all the causes he had publicly championed. After the immediate horrors of the Restoration years, there followed assiduous and effective persecution of a broad spectrum of Puritan and radical religious dissent. We saw in the last chapter the Quakerish orientation of Milton's tracts of 1659. He counted several active Quakers among his circle of closest friends in the 1660s. Quakers were treated especially badly for much of the period; droves were incarcerated; very many (although not his known Quaker friends) died of jail-fever in the insanitary and overcrowded hellholes of the English penal system. Presbyterians and other Puritan moderates had collaborated with the initiative to bring the King home, but from 1662 onward they too fell foul of a new Act of Uniformity, and their ministers were expelled from their livings in large numbers.

For a while it seemed that the restored ascendancy was irresistible. Certainly in *Paradise Lost,* Milton's lamentations for the godly in the fallen world are suffused with his sense of the extreme vulnerability of Puritans and radicals in the 1660s (the passage comes in Michael's account to Adam of what suffering awaits those who strive for salvation):

> Spiritual laws by carnal power shall force
> On every conscience; laws which none shall find
> Left them enrolled, or what the Spirit within
> Shall on the heart engrave. . . .

> Whence heavy persecution shall arise
> On all who in the worship persevere
> Of spirit and truth; the rest, far greater part,
> Well deem in outward rites and specious forms
> Religion satisfied; truth shall retire . . . .
>   so shall the world go on,
> To good malignant, to bad men benign. (XII, 521–38)

Given the genre in which he wrote and the kinds of hostile press control that prevailed (similar in many ways to that of the Laudian era), Milton's oblique comments are suprisingly easy to interpret in the context of the 1660s. Note that the horrors he defines relate, not to political systems and abstract principles of constitutionality, but to that most intimate of freedoms, the freedom of conscience.

Michael's advice to Adam was Milton's own policy in that grim decade: he should find an interior solace, "A paradise within thee, happier far" (*Paradise Lost,* XII, 587). But in the early 1670s, the Puritans' spiritual environment changed very significantly. In part this change came from a recognition, among those still persevering, that the enemy probably had done the worst he would do and they had survived. In part, it came from new initiatives in government policy that experimented with domestic policy as a concomitant of a new boldness in foreign affairs. In 1667 Charles II had been constrained in the aftermath of naval catastrophe to conclude his first Dutch war with a disadvantageous treaty; by 1670 he was engaged in attempts to reestablish England's international status through closer and clandestine cooperation with Louis XIV of France. He concluded a secret pact that offered him direct subsidies in return for military support against the Dutch and for an undertaking "to work toward the reestablishment of Roman Catholicism in England," which included, at some future point, a declaration of his own conversion.[2] Charles's mother was a Catholic; his brother and heir apparent, James Duke of York, the future James II, was a Catholic; so too was Lord Clifford, his Lord Treasurer. Meanwhile, others among his closest ministers were advocates of a more tolerant approach to Puritan dissent, arguing that persecution created unnecessary tensions. Indeed, in the late 1660s Charles did toy with some amelioration of the dissenters' condition in an unsustained way. He was persuaded to effect a bold measure designed to settle domestic discord about religion and to ease the position of his Catholic supporters as an adjunct to an Anglo-French attack on the United Provinces. However, although he enjoyed a good relationship throughout 1670–1671 with the current Parliament, the so-called Cavalier Parliament,[3] there would have been no majority there for moderation of measures against either dissenters or Catholics, so an extraparliamentary measure was necessary. Two days before declaring war, Charles issued a royal proclamation, the Declaration of Indulgence, which disabled anti-Catholic legislation and permitted dissenters to meet in worship on the issue of a license.

Milton's tract engages the parliamentary furor that ensued a little further down the road. The war had initially been popular, but it did not go especially well; moreover, it made Charles immediately and desperately dependent on Parliament for the approval of revenues to prosecute it effectively. There was some support for Parliamentary measures to retain the policies that tolerated Puritan dissent—it was obvious to many staunch Anglicans that penalizing otherwise law-abiding and passive citizens was counterproductive, but Catholicism retained its old stigma. The Parliamentary position was politically unassailable, and on 8 March, a week before Stavely's earliest date for the composition *Of True Religion,* "With his natural theatricality, [Charles] tore the seal from the Declaration [of Indulgence] with his own hands and broke it, and made sure that his servants informed both Houses of the fact," thus securing some temporary support although, as Hutton observes, this was "making the best of a terrible humiliation."[4]

The hero of Milton's *Samson Agonistes,* first published in 1671, had felt "Some rousing motions" (line 1382) with the return of his old powers. Milton, sensing perhaps a new strength in his enemies' palpable weakness, roused himself for one last effort in defense of the independency of the spirit within; the product is not a spectacle of mass destruction, but a cunning little tract as alert to audience and political context as any he had formerly written.

Milton simply plays the Catholic card. All Protestants share certain principles, although they differ on points that are not necessary for salvation. In contrast, Catholicism rejects the central tenets of Protestantism, which ground doctrine on the gospel and require each individual to take responsibility for his or her own faith; it claims control over the civil state; and its worship is idolatrous. Therefore, Milton claims, all Protestantism should be tolerated, whereas "Popery, as being Idolatrous, is not to be tolerated either in Public or in Private" (*CPW,* VIII, 431).

Milton plays for the support of the Church of England, praising where he can some of the Thirty-Nine Articles as manifesting "good and

Religious Reason" (*CPW,* VIII, 419), and he cleverly weaves aspects of Calvinism and Lutheranism into his list of "the hottest disputes among Protestants":

> The Lutheran holds Consubstantiation; an error indeed, but not mortal. The Calvinist is taxt with Predestination, and to make God the Author of sin; not with any dishonourable thought of God, but it may be over zealously asserting his absolute power, not without plea of Scripture. The Anabaptist is accus'd of Denying Infants their right to Baptism; again they say, they deny nothing but what the Scripture denies them. The Arian and Socinian are charg'd to dispute against the Trinity: they affirm to believe the Father, Son, and Holy Ghost, according to Scripture, and the Apostolic Creed; as for terms of Trinity, Triniunity, Coessentiality, Tripersonality, and the like, they reject them as Scholastic Notions, not to be found in Scripture. (*CPW,* VIII, 424–25)

So which of these disputed doctrines does Milton subscribe to? From the internal evidence of *Of True Religion* it is impossible to say, which rather confirms Milton's argument. These doctrines are technical issues to engage professional and amateur theologians and are embodied in terms of considerable opacity—hard, Latinate words like "consubstantiation" and "coessentiality," the stuff of footnotes. Those Protestants who work on such controversies, if they do so in godly fashion, staying close to the scriptural text, praying, waiting on the spirit, are "painful [i.e., painstaking] and zealous labourers"; but they cannot all be right. On points of controversy, someone must be in error. But such errors are not "damnable" and they do not prevent those laborers' personal salvation, because the saving tenets of Protestant faith are few and clearly based on plain gospel texts (*CPW,* VIII, 426).

From the antiprelatical texts onward, Milton had sought to associate his vision of true religion with images of clarity and simplicity, in contrast with the obscuring accretions of Catholic and episcopal theology. That same symbolic system still prevails: "I will not now enter into the Labyrinth of Councels and Fathers, an intangl'd wood which the Papist loves to fight in"; in contrast, "True Religion is the true Worship and Service of God, learnt and believed from the Word of God only" (*CPW,* VIII, 418, 419). As in his earliest tracts, Milton tries to speak for a wide spectrum of Protestant believers; here, he tries to address an even wider consensus. The question of what should be done about Catholicism becomes a question of what "we" should do about it:

> But if they who dissent in matters not essential to belief, while the common adversary [Catholicism] is in the field, shall stand jarring and pelting at one another, they will be soon routed and subdued. The Papist with open mouth makes much advantage of our several opinions; not that he is able to confute the worst of them, but that we by our continual jangle among our selves make them worse then they are indeed. To save our selves therefore, and resist the common enemy, it concerns us mainly to agree within our selves, that with joynt forces we may not only hold our own, but get ground; and why should we not? (*CPW*, VIII, 436)

He seems to relish that language of "we" and "us" that safely encircles Puritan dissent within the larger Protestant community. As for the Catholics, the state may defend itself by any means necessary, and their ceremonial practices are idolatrous and thus beyond toleration:

> Are we to punish them by corporal punishment, or fines in their Estates, upon account of their Religion? I suppose it stands not with the Clemency of the Gospel, more then what appertains to the security of the State: But first we must remove their Idolatry, and all the furniture thereof, whether Idols, or the Mass wherein they adore their God under Bread and Wine. (*CPW*, VIII, 431–32)

So clemency requires that they not be punished purely for their beliefs; but they may be punished if they attempt to worship as they would, and they may be punished insofar as their beliefs compromise the integrity of the Protestant nation state through loyalty to the Vatican. Not because of their beliefs but because of their practices and their internationalism Catholics may indeed be suppressed by the civil magistrate.

Milton's attack on Catholicism on the familiar Protestant argument that it erodes loyalty contrasts sharply with the assiduous way in which he avoids the political dangers some perceived in Puritan dissent. Charles I had suppressed Puritanism in the 1630s because he had a vision of a national church of a hierarchical and ceremonial kind; Charles II suppressed it in the 1660s because it was the religion of the Civil War rebels and because its adherents challenged his royal prerogative over the spiritual life of England. The "conventicles," or small groups in which Puritans characteristically met, were perceived as potentially subversive, the growth points for future rebellion or coups d'état, and senior civil servants like Sir Joseph Williamson (more on him shortly) assiduously kept files on sectaries and their meeting places.[5] Milton smartly displaces controversy and dissent within Protestantism away from the political domain, fixing it in the rarified exchanges of learned men grappling with issues like the characteristics of the Trinity.

Twenty years earlier Milton had been a government insider, drafting Latin letters of state on issues very similar to Charles II's negotiations with France and other countries. Now an outsider, he nevertheless judges well the political mood of the country. The same session that forced Charles to withdraw the Declaration of Indulgence passed the Test Act, which imposed on all officeholders "a declaration which no Catholic could accept."[6] By summer the legislation had flushed out the Duke of York and Lord Clifford from their clandestine Catholicism and precipitated their resignation from all public offices. Hounding the Duke became an obsession of subsequent sessions of Charles's Parliaments, provoking the dangerous "Exclusion Crisis" of the late 1670s and early 1680s, which came close to forcing James's exclusion from succession and the promotion of the claims of one of Charles's illegimitate sons, James, Duke of Monmouth, as a Protestant alternative. That same rabid anti-Catholic sentiment stimulated the ill-judged Monmouth rebellion against the reign of James II and the eventual displacement of James by William of Orange in the so-called Glorious Revolution of 1688–1690, almost bloodless in England, although a rather gorier transition in Ireland.

Letters Patents, Textbooks, and Histories

Milton toward the end of his life developed concerns and strategies that brought him back into the reviving body of anticourt political activists, the group that would emerge shortly as the Whigs. Sensabaugh in his classic study demonstrates the posthumous role of Milton's writing as an oeuvre of political thought and sentiment open to Whig appropriation. More recently, von Maltzahn has revisited the subject, identifying both a diversity of Whig responses to the Miltonic legacy and a new and early potency for his radical prose.[7] Indeed, as von Maltzahn argues, Milton's last lifetime publication, a translation rather than a work of controversy, should be contextualized in a renewed interest in the constitutional basis of the Stuart monarchy.[8] The text in question is *A Declaration, or Letters Patents of the Election of this present King of Poland* John the Third, *Elected on the 22d of May last past,* Anno Dom. *1674,* published three or four months before Milton's death in November 1674. Milton in his civil service career had translated such documents professionally, and obviously had the expertise to produce an English version of the Latin account published by the Polish government to describe the election of the redoubtable Jan Sobieski. Two aspects made the account politically significant. The Polish monarchy had an elective basis, which meant that an unsatisfactory person—someone like James, Duke of York, for example—ought never to be crowned. The second point, which adds a certain frisson, is that Sobieski (like Cromwell) was an extraordinarily successful general in the national interest, having scored spectacular victories over Turks, Tartars, and Cossacks, "hazarding his life devoted to God and his Countrey" (*CPW,* VIII, 449)—unlike the Duke of York, for example, who as commander of the English fleet had blundered frequently in the opening years of the second Dutch War. Milton, of course, does not make the points explicitly, but, recontextualized in the crises of the early 1670s, his translation functions as a sharp reminder of constitutional alternatives.

We turn now to his remaining lifetime publications of the post-Restoration period. Some need not detain us long. In 1669 he published *Accedence Commenc't Grammar, Supply'd with sufficient Rules, For the use of such (Younger or Elder) as are desirous, without more trouble than need to attain the* Latin Tongue; *The Elder sort especially, with little Teaching, and their own Industry.* This publication is simply a primer of Latin grammar, explaining the inflectional system with some more rudimentary accounts of larger syntactical features. Many such books existed, some somewhat longer and most written in Latin. Milton, by using English for the explanatory and instructional material and by striving for brevity, attempts a user-friendliness that accords with the pedagogic functionalism that he advocated in *Of Education,* and the book's composition may well date from the early 1640s when Milton was directly involved in the education of his nephews. This assumption seems probable but has no supporting evidence. Interestingly, the title page offers the work both as a possible course-book for the young and as a self-study guide for more mature students; using it, one could certainly develop an adequate understanding of Latin grammar, although one would have to look elsewhere for assistance with vocabulary acquisition. I am aware of nothing innovative in Milton's account of Latin syntax.

His other educational publication of the period is *Joannis Miltoni Angli, Artis Logicæ Plenior Institutio, Ad* Petri Rami *Methodum concinnata* [*A Fuller Course in the Art of Logic Conformed to the Method of* Peter Ramus] (1672). The Latin medium indicates a text for more advanced students and possibly addresses a potentially international market. Again, no evidence exists, but scholars usually hypothesize an early date of composition. Whereas Milton's *Accedence Commenc't Grammar* depends on a long tradition of other such primers, his *Logic* is really a Miltonic adaptation of George Downame's *Commentarii in P. Rami* (Frankfurt, 1601), together with almost all of Ramus's Latin *Dialectic* in its final edition (1572). As Walter J. Ong explains, this is a deeply derivative book:

> In verbatim quotations the principle Milton generally follows is to iden-
> tify the source of the quotation in every case except where the quotation
> is simply Ramus's text itself, in which case it is simply italicized without
> any attribution, or from Downame, in which case it is normally neither
> put in italics nor indentified as Downame's in any way at all. Milton, in
> other words, simply appropriates much of Downame's text as though it
> were his own.[9]

Downame's commentary had sought to make Ramist principles clearer by illustration from classical and postclassical Greek and Latin authors; Milton's editorial intervention into Downame's work removes postclassical exemplars and adds classical examples of his own. The resulting text nicely illustrates differences between early modern and late-twentieth-century notions of authorship. Were an academic to proceed nowadays as Milton did, the charges of plagiarism would be irresistible; tenure would be lost; dismissal would follow. But the sort of gradual and partial transformation—very largely unacknowledged, for Downame is mentioned only once—points to a radically different conceptual framework, one in which it is legitimate to take a good book, make it better, and pass it on as one's own. Had Milton's practice seemed shameful in his own day, he had enemies in large numbers who would have said so. The book that results is a curiously layered text, incorporating Ramus's original propositions and Downame's explanations and exemplification, filtered through Miltonic criteria of neoclassical correctness and variously altered by Milton, perhaps through the incorporation of other commentaries that have not consistently been identified. The result is a lucid and not uninterestingly exemplified account of a major influence on the intellectual climate of Milton's own day, a genuinely useful introduction to the art of logic as it was contemporaneously understood. But is it Milton's? The question will recur when we consider *De Doctrina Christiana*.

Milton also wrote two histories and a historical digression. The most ambitious appeared in 1671 under the title *The History of Britain, That part especially now called England. From The first Traditional Beginning, Continued to the Norman Conquest. Collected out of the Antientest and best Authors thereof,* although the date of its composition remains a matter of debate. It runs to more than three hundred quarto pages, almost half as long again as *Eikonoklastes.* Although lately this book has been the subject of some intelligent scholarship, it remains a relatively unexplored and somewhat unengaging text.[10] As with his expeditions into Latin grammar and into logic, Milton's scholarly achievements should not be overstated. Von Maltzahn summarizes the issues:

> Milton seems to have viewed the demands of writing the *History* lightly. Milton knew his sources thoroughly after fifteen years of intermittent study. . . . After all, Book I was just a condensed version of Geoffrey of Monmouth's prehistory, Book III a swift collation chiefly of Bede, Gildas, Nennius, and Malmesbury, and Book IV of Bede, Malmesbury, and the *Anglo-Saxon Chronicle.*[11]

Among Milton's contemporaries, several scholarly antiquaries—going beyond the received and printed tradition—were establishing the discipline of English historical research.[12] Milton did not belong to this vanguard; as von Maltzahn concludes, "His research . . . does not go beyond printed sources; his humanist preoccupation with narratives bears little comparison with the masterly scholarship of a Selden or a Spelman."[13]

Nor do those narratives always sustain interest. Much of the history Milton relates is inconsequential, for the sources are too fragmentary and too underdeveloped to support an account that can sustain interest. At times, a bored Milton realizes he is in danger of boring his readers and attempts a sort of preemptive apology:

> I am sensible how wearisom it may likely be to read of so many bare and reasonless Actions, so many names of Kings one after another, acting little more then mute persons in a Scene: what would it be to have inserted the long Bead-roll of Archbishops, Bishops, Abbots, Abbesses, and thir doeings, neither to Religion profitable nor to morality, swelling my Authors each to a voluminous body, by me studiously omitted. (*CPW,* V.i, 239)

Milton concedes that parts of the narrative are boring, but not as boring as they would have been if he had not "studiously" cut out the real dross.

His account, however, is by no means ideologically transparent; rather, he suffuses the work with characteristic Miltonic values, particularly a recurrent and obtrusive anticlericalism. He persistently trashes his sources in terms that highlight their monkish ignorance and their partiality to self-interest disguised as piety:

> Henceforth [that is, after the Romans leave and Roman historians no longer comment on Britain] we are to stear by another sort of Authors; neer anough to the things they write, as in thir own Countrie, if that would serve; in time not much belated, some of equal age; in expression barbarous; and to say how judicious, I suspend a while: this we must expect; in civil matters to find them dubious Relaters, and still to the best advantage of what they term holy Church, meaning indeed themselves: in most other matters of Religion, blind, astonish'd, and strook with superstition as with a Planet; in one word, Monks. (*CPW,* V.i, 127–28)

There are fascinating narratives to be found in such sources, but Milton declines to accept what cannot be reconciled to reason. The incorporeal figure of Arthur passes lightly over his pages, leaving a shallow trace in the dust of history: "He who can accept of Legends for good story, may quickly swell a volume with trash" (*CPW,* V.i, 166). Even Arthur's most signal accomplishment as described in the medieval chronicles, the victory at Badon Hill, is dubiously ascribed to him (*CPW,* V.i, 166). But the clergy of earlier days have other faults besides credulousness or mendacity, according to Milton, faults that find expression in terms redolent of his excoriation of the clergy of his own age:

> Unlerned, Unapprehensive, yet impudent; suttle Prowlers, Pastors in Name, but indeed Wolves; intent upon all occasions, not to feed the Flock, but to pamper and well line themselves: not call'd, but seising on the Ministry as a Trade, not as a Spiritual Charge: teaching the people, not by sound Doctrine, but by evil Example. (*CPW,* V.i, 175)

The idiom accords well with a Miltonic voice heard in unbroken antipathy to the professional clergy from "Lycidas" through the antiprelatical pamphlets to the texts of 1659.

Milton's *History* is almost a text without heroes (Alfred and his immediate successors receive a sympathetic account). Milton surveys the peoples trooping over the British landscape in the dark ages and finds them all wanting. The British, primitive before the Romans come, are effete and incapable of taking the opportunities afforded them by their departure; Saxons and Danes and Normans are utterly "barbarous" (*CPW,* V.i, 257–58). Interestingly, Milton declines to follow many contemporary radicals in attributing to Saxon society a sort of utopian status perverted

by a Norman Conquest that established monarchy as the Stuarts understood it, what is sometimes called the myth of the Norman Yoke.[14] For
the most part, Milton's pre-Conquest Britain is populated with uncul-
tured savages engaged in mindless strife, gross atrocities, and various
sexual depravities (usually, but not always, involving incest); scarcely a
paradigm for a modern state:

> The great men giv'n to gluttony and dissolute life, made a prey of the
> common people, abuseing thir Daughters whom they had in service, then
> turning them off to the Stews, the meaner sort tipling together night and
> day, spent all they had in Drunk'ness, attended with other Vices which
> effeminate mens minds. Whence it came to pass, that carried on with fury
> and rashness more then any true fortitude or skill of War, they gave to
> *William* thir Conqueror so easie a Conquest. (*CPW,* V.i, 402–3)

Obliquely, though, another very subversive political thesis does emerge:
that kingship—which the Stuarts and their apologists would represent
as an immutable and divinely sanctioned governmental system for the
Britain of the three kingdoms of England (with Wales), Scotland, and
Ireland—is a highly unstable constitutional phenomenon with a decid-
edly unprovidential early history, as kings and kingdoms rise and fall in
vast profusion, especially in the early Saxon period.

Occasionally in the published *History,* Milton draws explicit points of
analogy with his own age. When Bede remarks that the Irish were "a
harmless Nation . . . and ever friendly to the English," Milton with
obvious reference to the uprising of 1641 and subsequent events in Ireland adds "in both which they seem to have left a posterity much unlike
them at this day" (*CPW,* V.i, 222). It is known that the censor took a
close interest in Milton's text, and other passages touching on contemporary affairs may well have been excised.[15] By far the most interesting
digression on this history of his own age was first printed in 1681 under
the title *Mr John Miltons Character of the Long Parliament and Assembly of
Divines in MDCXLI. Omitted in his other Works, and never before Printed,
And very seasonable for these times.*

Again, von Maltzahn has perceptively engaged the issues.[16] The
pamphlet—a mere 12 pages—was published by Henry Brome, a bookseller strongly associated with Roger L'Estrange, longtime adversary of
Milton and the censor who controlled the press at the time *The History*
was published in 1670. Strikingly, Milton's Whig biographers do not
mention the pamphlet in their posthumous accounts of him, as though

it is ideologically embarrassing as indeed it is because it is deeply critical of the Long Parliament. The text is "very seasonable for these times" in 1681 only if one is a Tory supporter of the King and the Duke of York against attempts to exclude the latter from the royal succession, and it is seasonable because it shows the precursors of the Whigs to have been rogues and incompetents. Most probably, Milton, realizing 1670 was not a time during which to give comfort to his enemies, had cut the digression himself when he sent *The History* to the press. L'Estrange had then acquired a copy of the digression—quite possibly from Sir Joseph Williamson, who had searched through Milton's literary remains shortly after his death and could well have ordered a transcription[17]—and had put out the 1681 version of the digression through the agency of his usual publisher at the point at which the pamphlet may have been expected to damage the Whig cause most.

Milton probably intended to append to his discussion of the short-comings of the British after the Roman withdrawal a radical critique of the failings of the Long Parliament. His comments are wholly unsurprising in the sense that, since the mid-1640s and the attack on his divorce tracts, he had been deeply critical of the Presbyterian clergy favored by the Long Parliament and because his own public career was as a servant of the purged Parliament and the protectorate, both of which owed their being to the exclusion of the Presbyterian majority in the Long Parliament. Of course he thought that both clergy and laity were scoundrels and incompetents. But it would have been profitless to say so in 1670; nor, presumably, would he have wanted his withdrawn digression to see light of day during the Exclusion Crisis. L'Estrange rather smartly hijacked a radical text probably written by Milton in the late 1640s to use against the radicals of the 1680s.

A Brief History of Moscovia: and Of other less-known Countries lying eastward of Russia *as far as* Cathay. *Gather'd from the Writings of several Eye-witnesses,* Milton's remaining historical treatise, was also published posthumously, in 1682, although for this text we need suspect no conspiracies. The publisher, Brabazon Aylmer, explains the delay in his "Advertisement":

> This book was writ by the Authour's own hand, before he lost his sight. And sometime before his death dispos'd of it to be printed. But it being small, the Bookseller hop'd to have procured some other suitable Piece of the same Authour's to have joyn'd with it, or else it had been publish'd 'ere now. (*CPW*, VIII, 475)

Aylmer had published a double volume of Milton's familiar letters and his *Prolusions* in 1674, the publication of which was also delayed while the publisher sought to acquire state papers to make a better collection; so if he were hunting around for something a bit more marketable to put with *Moscovia,* he would merely have been following a commercial practice he had used before. In any event, Aylmer settled for publishing this hundred-page octavo.

His account of its origins is not improbable. George Parks, its editor, remarks that it remains "more akin to a foreign-office briefing than to a book,"[18] and possibly Milton may first have assembled this account in the context of preparing a brief for a republican diplomatic mission. Certainly, his narrative of the odd ways in which Russian leaders had formerly conducted themselves with respect to foreign envoys would have been quite useful.

As Parks notes, Milton depends very largely on just two sources (there is nothing firsthand in his account): Richard Hakluyt's *Principal Navigations, Voyages, Traffiques, and Discoveries of the English Nation* (1598–1600) and Samuel Purchas's *Purchas His Pilgrimes* (1625).[19] Milton's choice of material occasionally reflects a familiar Miltonic agenda, as in his anecdotes to the discredit of the Russian clergy:

> they observe 4 Lents, have Service in their Churches daily, from two hours before dawn to Evening; yet for Whordom, Drunkenness and Extortion none worse than the Clergy. (*CPW,* VIII, 492)

One detail, for which Parks has not found a source, relates to Russian divorce practice: "Upon utter dislike, the Husband divorces; which Liberty no doubt they receiv'd first with their Religion from the *Greek* Church, and the Imperial Laws" (*CPW,* VIII, 493–94). Of course, Milton is drawn to demonstrating that practices other than the current English laws prevail elsewhere, but because Russian husbands, on his account, usually whip their wives at least weekly (*CPW,* VIII, 493), he is scarcely advancing Russian customs as an ideal to be followed.

The State Papers and *De Doctrina Christiana*

We turn now to consider *De Doctrina Christiana.* The manuscript, PRO SP 9/61, was discovered in 1823 by Robert Lemon Sr., Deputy Keeper of His Majesty's State Papers, in a "press" (that is, a large cupboard) in the Old State Paper Office, Whitehall, in immediate proximity to a collection of transcriptions of Milton's State Papers (now in the Public Record Office and catalogued as PRO SP 9/194), which are in the same hand as that responsible for the first part of *De Doctrina Christiana*. The treatise was wrapped in a sort of parchment envelope addressed "To Mr. Skinner, Mercht."

It is known that SP 9/61 and SP 9/194 were placed in the State Paper Office by Sir Joseph Williamson, probably in 1677. They had been supplied to him by Daniel Skinner Jr. at Williamson's insistence. Our only account of the origins of Williamson's involvement comes from a letter written by Skinner to the diarist and civil servant Samuel Pepys, dating probably from the autumn of 1676 or from early in 1677. Skinner, as will emerge, was a man of dubious probity, and some of the letter's comments are part of an account in which he explains his current indigence, his future prospects, and asks for a loan of £10 from Pepys, who knew Skinner, apparently, because he was the brother of Mary Skinner, one of Pepys's mistresses. Skinner says that he approached Williamson "to acquaint him that there was a book come about against his authority" and to ask that Williamson grant Skinner a license to print his own version of the book or else that Williamson suppress the book and allow Skinner to advertise that his own version was being printed in Amsterdam.[20]

It is possible that Skinner was as ingenuous or inept as he seems in his dealing with Williamson. Williamson evidently summoned him, and after interrogation, Skinner wrote a statement in his own hand and signed it. The document, dated 18 October 1676 in a different hand, testifies that "4 or 5 moneths agoe ... Mr. Pitts Bookseller of Pauls Churchyard," hearing that Skinner had some of Milton's state papers and that Skinner had "long before committed the true perfect copy of the state letters" to Elzevir, a publisher in Amsterdam, had met with Skinner to propose that an arrangement should be brokered with Elzevir that would give the latter access to whatever papers Pitts had that Elzevir was missing. According to Skinner's account, he advised Pitts that it was improbable that Elzevir would concur, and Pitts declared he would "proceed his own way and make the best advantage of 'em." Skinner ends his attestation noting that "Mr. Pitts has been the man by whose meanes this late imperfect surreptitious copy, has been publisht."[21]

Skinner is speaking of state papers, but in much of the correspondence that is extant, which involves Skinner Jr., his father, Daniel Skinner Sr., and Daniel Elzevir, it is clear that Skinner had sent both papers and treatise to Elzevir and that both were returned to him through the agency of his father—the Daniel Skinner, Merchant, of the now lost envelope—so the presence of the two documents together in the State Paper Office is wholly explained. Williamson evidently both terrified Skinner Jr. (as well he might) and excited him with the prospect of some advancement. Elzevir's letter to Skinner Sr. is an assurance that he will return the manuscript material as the son had requested and a later letter confirms that he has done that.[22]

Meanwhile, Williamson remained actively concerned about the fate of the Miltonic state papers that had been in the possession of Moses Pitt (as he is usually known). We are unaware of any further action taken against Pitt, who enjoyed considerable success as a bookseller, particularly in the early 1680s.[23] But presumably the papers that Skinner says Pitt had possessed provided the copy for *Literae Pseudo-senatus Anglicani,* the collection of Miltonic state papers published in two editions in 1676. Neither edition mentions place of publication, bookseller, or printer. On 19 January 1677, Williamson wrote to Roger Meredith, secretary to the Embassy to the United Provinces and his principal information gatherer on Dutch affairs, that "His Majtie's informed of a pernicious Book of that late Villain Milton's, now about to be printed at Leyden, I am commanded to signify to you, that you immediately apply yr selfe, to find out by the best means you may, if there be any such, who's the printer, and by what order he is sett on worke." He went on to say that there is "one Skinner" that "some time since did owne to have had such a thing in his intentions, but being made sensible, as he seemed to be, of the danger he ranne into, in haveing a hand in any such thing, he promised for ever to lay aside the thought of it, and even to give up his copy, I know not whether this may be the same thing."[24] Meredith had initial problems with his agent at Leyden and found nothing there; eventually, though, he sent Williamson an unspecified volume, supplied to him by his bookseller in Amsterdam and printed about "three months since" (he writes in February 1677). This would seem to be a copy of the *Literae Pseudo-senatus Anglicani,* perhaps indeed supplied from an Amsterdam press.[25]

It is clear that Williamson thought he had scared young Skinner quite well but still did not trust him; it is further clear that Williamson expected and was monitoring a plurality of Miltonic state papers and was considerably concerned about suppressing them. It was part of Williamson's portfolio of responsibilities to gather up state documents from the Interregnum. Such correspondence, reflecting a highly successful period of English involvement in Continental power politics, most certainly threw into sharp relief the incompetencies and duplicities that characterized Charles II's prosecution of his own Dutch wars and the junior role Charles was obliged to play to Louis XIV.

No doubt with some satisfaction, Williamson lodged the confiscated papers eventually given him by the Skinners in the State Paper Office, another stake through the wandering spirit of that late villain. Indeed, even though Williamson's concern was primarily with the state papers, he may well have felt some satisfaction in burying the treatise too. We know from Skinner's letter to Pepys that Williamson had looked at other Miltonic papers in Skinner's possession and returned them to Skinner; so those papers, evidently, did not merit the treatment that the treatise received. By 1677, the issue seemed to have been resolved to Williamson's satisfaction, and so it remained until 1823. On their rediscovery, the treatise and the state papers were accepted as authentically Miltonic, almost without demur. In the middle and later twentieth century, the treatise has posed a considerable interpretative challenge, especially for the study of Milton's epics. Whereas some scholars, such as Barbara Lewalski in her work on *Paradise Regained* and Maurice Kelley in *This Great Argument* have, in Kelley's phrase, taken the treatise as a "gloss" on uncertainties and ambiguities in the poetical oeuvre, others, such as C. A. Patrides and William Hunter in his earlier phase, conscious of disparities between the treatise and poems, have sought to explain those inconsistencies in terms of differences of genre and situation. However, since 1991, Hunter has questioned the provenance of the treatise in a series of essays and conference papers.[26]

At the present time, three hypotheses are current. The first accepts the traditional attribution. The treatise is evidently the work of someone of radical theological outlook who is both an Arminian (as Milton certainly was) and, apparently, an advocate of divorce reform (as, again, Milton certainly was). The manuscript was in Milton's possession at his death and no one else has been identified who was both Arminian and a divorce reformer. So why dispute the traditional and obviously correct attribution?[27]

The second hypothesis, associated most strongly with Hunter, recognizes that the early history of the manuscript is sufficiently uncertain for some doubt to be entertained. The hypothesis invokes long-felt anxieties about apparent discrepancies between the theology of *Paradise Lost,* in particular, and the theology of *De Doctrina Christiana*. The most significant problems relate to the depiction of the relationship between the Father and the Son, which in the epic may be interpreted as not radically remote from Protestant Trinitarian orthodoxy but which in the treatise subordinates the role of the Son in heretical ways. There are numerous minor discrepancies as well. Moreover, the commonsense argument is that a blind man could not have written an exegetical treatise that contains, as *De Doctrina Christiana* does, more than nine thousand biblical references.[28] The second hypothesis resolves these problems by dismissing the Miltonic provenance, arguing instead that the treatise was simply in Milton's possession, that it was composed by someone else but that Milton found it useful to draw on.

The third hypothesis, to which I currently subscribe, postulates a process of composition analogous to that of Milton's *Logic*. The hypothesis is based on a close consideration of the physical characteristics of the manuscript and on a stylometric analysis.[29] The former indicates that PRO SP 9/61 is a working manuscript of a text that is in the process of revision. Different chapters seem to be left at rather different stages. The manuscript has been organized to allow new material to be added more easily. Stylometrics is the science of measuring stylistic variables in texts. It is a branch of statistics that aims to identify an author's stylistic preferences, rather like a fingerprint that he or she leaves on whatever is written. In the case of *De Doctrina Christiana,* there is evidence that some sections are much closer to Milton's characteristic practice than others. What evidence there is suggests first that Milton was engaged in the process of revising a treatise, a process either set aside or interrupted by his death, and second, that the basis of his treatise was some other treatise, or treatises, that he was adding to, deleting from, and in other ways transforming, rather as he transformed Downame's text in preparing the *Logic*. If the third hypothesis is right, *De Doctrina Christiana* is and is not Miltonic, nor can we be sure which parts were endorsed by Milton as the explicit statement of true doctrine because the transformation was not completed at his death.

So whatever the fascinations and interpretative challenges posed by *De Doctrina Christiana,* its status within the Milton oeuvre is likely to remain contested and uncertain for some time to come. Its use as an interpretative key to the certainly canonical works should be approached with caution.

But we do not need this treatise to know that Milton in his age wrote bold, brave, original, and oppositional works. His last and greatest poems, *Paradise Lost, Paradise Regained,* and *Samson Agonistes,* celebrate the resistance of the godly, and the first of these offers the most profound and complex vision of the godhead found in seventeenth-century

England. Milton's reputation and, more significantly, the responses he elicited indicate his impact on his age. His divorce tracts placed him outside the pale of Puritan respectability; his was the most eloquent voice in defense of regicide and republicanism before England and before the world; he was among the last defenders of the Good Old Cause; in the Restoration, he endured prosecution and suspicion until circumstances permitted one last blast of his trumpet; even in death his literary legacy was hunted out and suppressed. A Miltonic provenance for *De Doctrina Christiana* is surely not essential for the demonstration of Milton's abiding radicalism.

Notes and References

Chapter One

1. The best source of biographical information is William Riley Parker, *Milton: A Biography and a Biographical Commentary,* 2 vols., 2d ed., revised by Gordon Campbell (Oxford: Clarendon Press, 1996). See also J. Milton French, *The Life Records of John Milton,* 5 vols. (New Brunswick: Rutgers University Press, 1949–1958; reprint, New York: Gordian Press, 1966) and Gordon Campbell, *A Milton Chronology* (London and Basingstoke: Macmillan; Lanham: Barnes and Noble, 1997). In recent years, our knowledge, especially of Milton's career in the civil service, has been considerably augmented by Leo Miller, *John Milton and the Oldenburg Safeguard: New Light on Milton and his Friends in the Commonwealth from the Diaries and Letters of Hermann Mylius, Agonist in the Early History of Modern Diplomacy* (New York: Loewenthal Press, 1985) and Robert T. Fallon, *Milton in Government* (University Park: Pennsylvania State University Press, 1993).

2. See, most recently, John T. Shawcross, *John Milton: The Self and the World* (Lexington: University of Kentucky Press, 1993), which rests heavily on twentieth-century psychoanalytical assumptions.

Chapter Two

1. French, II, 140.

2. He presented to George Thomason a copy of *Areopagitica,* which is extant in the British Library and which bears a title-page inscription indicating that it was a gift from the author (French, II, 113). Thomason collected nearly all Milton's publications, and many of them may well have been gifts. Milton gave a bound set of his early tracts to the Keeper of the King's Library (French, II, 125–26).

3. See, for example, the comments he makes on the author of *A Modest Confutation of a Slanderous and Scurrilous Libell, Entituled, Animadversions* (London, 1642) in *An Apology Against a Pamphlet Call'd A Modest Confutation, CPW,* I, 894. See also Thomas N. Corns, "New Light on the Left Hand: Contemporary Views of Milton's Prose Style," *Durham University Journal* 72 (1980): 177–81.

4. John Cleveland, *John Cleaveland Revived: Poems, Orations, Epistles* (1659, and frequently reprinted); see also David Masson, *The Life of John Milton* (1881; reprint, Gloucester, Mass.: Peter Smith, 1965), I, 297.

5. "The Printer's Preface to the Reader," *Milton: Private Correspondence and Academic Exercises,* translated from the Latin by Phyllis B. Tillyard with an

introduction and commentary by E. M. W. Tillyard (Cambridge: Cambridge University Press, 1932), 3.

6. John Milton, *Literae Pseudo-senatus Anglicani* (Amsterdam, 1676, 2 eds.).

7. *Correspondence and Exercises,* 3.

8. Ibid., ix.

9. Masson, *Life,* I, 274.

10. Ibid., 275.

11. E. M. W. Tillyard in *Correspondence and Exercises,* xxiv.

12. See Thomas N. Corns, *Uncloistered Virtue: English Political Literature, 1640–1660* (Oxford: Clarendon Press, 1992), 55, n. 37.

Chapter Three

1. For the most recent summary of the life records, see Gordon Campbell, *A Milton Chronology* (London and Basingstoke: Macmillan; Lanham: Barnes and Noble, 1997). For attempts to read *A Masque* as an oppositional or radical document, see David Norbrook, *Poetry and Politics in the English Renaissance* (London: Routledge and Kegan Paul, 1984), 235–85 and especially 245–65; Michael Wilding, *Dragons Teeth: Literature in the English Revolution* (Oxford: Clarendon Press, 1987), 7–27.

2. The Licensing Order of 1637.

3. This account owes much to Kevin Sharpe's richly detailed study, *The Personal Rule of Charles I* (New Haven and London: Yale University Press, 1992).

4. Nicholas Tyacke's fullest rehearsal of the argument that the troubles within the Church originated in the rise of Arminianism is *Anti-Calvinists: The Rise of English Arminianism, c. 1590–1640* (Oxford: Clarendon Press, 1987).

5. Sharpe, *Personal Rule,* chap. 6; Julian Davies, *The Caroline Captivity of the Church: Charles I and the Remolding of Anglicanism 1625–1641* (Oxford: Clarendon Press, 1992).

6. Sharpe, *Personal Rule,* 758–65.

7. Quoted by Sharpe, *Personal Rule,* 762, from a contemporary account; the victim here was Burton, but all three were equally brave.

8. John T. Shawcross, *Milton: The Self and the World* (Lexington: University of Kentucky Press, 1993), 88–89.

9. John Morrill, "The Religious Context of the English Civil War," *Transactions of the Royal Historical Society,* 5th series, 34 (1984); reprinted in John Morrill, *The Nature of the English Revolution* (London and New York: Longman, 1993), 47.

10. Stephen Marshall, Edmund Calamy, Thomas Young, Matthew Newcomen, and William (which gives the "double u") Spurstow; Thomas Young had been engaged as a part-time tutor to Milton when he was a schoolboy, and Milton had addressed a Latin poem to Young in the late 1620s.

11. Hall, *Humble Remonstrance*, 6.

12. This chronology follows the full account in *CPW*, I, 76–86.

13. *CPW*, I, 1012.

14. See Corns, "Milton's Antiprelatical Tracts and the Marginality of Doctrine," in *Heretical Milton*, ed. John Rumrich and Stephen Dobraski (Cambridge: Cambridge University Press, forthcoming).

15. *CPW*, I, 618–20 has a useful account, which I largely follow here.

16. Davies, *Caroline Captivity*, 51–54.

17. R. Buick Knox, *James Ussher Archbishop of Armagh* (Cardiff: University of Wales Press, 1967), 189.

18. Again I follow the *CPW* chronology (I, 653–54).

19. Again, *CPW* provides an account of its circumstances (I, 736–43).

20. Corns, *Uncloistered Virtue*, 34.

21. Christopher Hill, *The World Turned Upside Down: Radical Ideas During the English Revolution* (London: Maurice Temple Smith, 1972; Harmondsworth: Penguin, 1975), 317–18.

22. Hill, *World*, 27.

Chapter Four

1. See chapter 3.

2 French, II, 81; commentators on the document have noted that it may indicate not an obligation to bear arms in the royalist cause but to supply arms for others to bear.

3. Lawrence Stone, *The Family, Sex and Marriage In England 1500–1800* (London: Weidenfeld and Nicolson, 1977; Harmondsworth: Penguin, 1979), 411–12.

4. This account of the marriage largely follows Parker, *The Life of John Milton* (Oxford: Clarendon Press, 1968), I, 226–32.

5. Mary Nyquist, "The Genesis of Gendered Subjectivity in the Divorce Tracts and in *Paradise Lost*," *in Re-membering Milton; New Essays on the Texts and the Traditions*, ed. Mary Nyquist and Margaret W. Ferguson (London: Methuen, 1987; London: Methuen, 1988), 105.

6. See Keith Thomas, "The Puritans and Adultery: The Act of 1650 Reconsidered," in *Puritans and Revolutionaries*, ed. Donald Pennington and Keith Thomas (Oxford: Clarendon Press, 1978), 257–82. Interestingly, the legislation was passed after some of the more authoritarian and repressive members of Parliament had been excluded.

7. Stephen Fallon, "The Metaphysics of Milton's Divorce Tracts," in *Politics, Poetics, and Hermeneutics in Milton's Prose*, ed. David Loewenstein and James Grantham Turner (Cambridge: Cambridge University Press, 1990), 71; he is commenting on *Colasterion, CPW*, II, 740.

8. A mythical Etruscan despot who, according to Virgil, "would even link dead bodies with the living, fitting hand to hand and face to face . . . and,

in the oozy slime and poison of that dread embrace, thus slay them by a linger-ing death." (*CPW,* II, 327, n. 1).

9. See chapter 3.

10. The issues are singularly well analyzed by Ernest Sirluck, *CPW,* II, 107–45.

11. Penry Miller, *Roger Williams: His Contribution to the American Tradi-tion* (New York and Indianapolis: Bobbs-Merrill, 1953; New York: Atheneum, 1962), 101. For a fuller account of the Presbyterian conspiracy against Milton and of the evidence on which it is based, see Corns, *Uncloistered Virtue,* 51–55.

12. *CPW,* II, 51.

13. See Thomas N. Corns, *The Development of Milton's Prose Style* (Oxford: Clarendon Press, 1982), especially chap. 10.

14. Points made by Arnold Williams, editor, *CPW,* II, 418.

15. Once more I follow the dating of the *CPW* editors.

16. "Sonnet XI," lines 1–8, *Poems,* 305.

17. *Oxford English Dictionary,* 2d ed., s.v. "Tetrachord"; only one author is cited using the word before Milton.

18. On these and similar issues, see James Grantham Turner, *One Flesh: Paradisal Marriage and Sexual Relations in the Age of Milton* (Oxford: Clarendon Press, 1987; Oxford: Clarendon Press, 1993), especially 194–215.

19. *CPW,* II, 722, n. 1.

20. The Star Chamber Decree of 1637, item 2, *CPW,* II, 793–94.

21. The Licensing Order of 1643, *CPW,* II, 797–98.

22. Thomas N. Corns, "Publication and Politics, 1640–1661: An SPSS-Based Account of the Thomason Collection of Civil War Tracts," *Literary and Linguistic Computing* 1 (1986): 74–84.

23. Corns, ibid.

24. French, II, 116–17.

25. Stanley Fish, "Driving from the Letter: Truth and Indeterminacy in Milton's *Areopagitica,*" in Nyquist and Ferguson, *Re-membering Milton,* 238.

26. See chap. 2, n. 2 of this book.

27. Corns, "New Light."

28. Francis Bacon, *The Advancement of Learning,* ed. G. W. Kitchin (Lon-don and Toronto: JM Dent; New York: EP Dutton, 1915; reprint, London: Dent, 1965), 24.

Chapter Five

1. "On the New Forcers of Conscience under the Long Parliament," lines 1–6, *Poems,* 296; Carey tentatively dates the poem August 1646.

2. For a balanced account of the issues, see John Morrill, "The Army Revolt of 1647," reprinted in *The Nature of the English Revolution* (London and New York: Longman, 1993), 307–31. The view is most forcefully expressed in Mark A. Kishlansky, *The Rise of the New Model Army* (Cambridge: Cambridge

University Press, 1979); but for a counterblast, see Christopher Hill, *A Turbulent, Seditious, and Factious People: John Bunyan and his Church* (Oxford: Clarendon Press, 1988; Oxford: Oxford University Press, 1989), 381.

3. Morrill, "Revolt," 308.

4. David E. Underdown's study *Pride's Purge: Politics in the Puritan Revolution* (Oxford: Clarendon Press, 1971) remains the best account of these years.

5. "On the Lord General Fairfax at the seige of Colchester," lines 9–14, *Poems,* 322–23.

6. C. V. Wedgwood, *The Trial of Charles* (London: Collins, 1964; London: The Reprint Society, 1966), 13; Wedgwood's remains the most compelling narrative of the events.

7. On the undeveloped nature of English republican theory and Milton's relation to it, see Thomas N. Corns, "Milton and the Characteristics of a Free Commonwealth," in *Milton and Republicanism,* ed. David Armitage, Armand Hiny, and Quentin Skinner (Cambridge: Cambridge University Press, 1995), 25–42.

8. *An Agreement of the Free People of England, in Freedom in Arms: A Selection of Leveller Writings,* ed. A. L. Morton (London: Lawrence and Wishart, 1975), 268.

9. Blair Worden, *The Rump Parliament 1648–1653* (Cambridge: Cambridge University Press, 1974), 40; see also Corns, "Milton and the Characteristics," 27.

10. Worden, *Rump,* 42.

11. French, II, 234, 236.

12. Ibid., 240.

13. The relationship of the political and military issues in Ireland are well reviewed by Ian Gentles, *The New Model Army in England, Ireland, and Scotland, 1645–1653* (Oxford and Cambridge, Mass.: Blackwell, 1992), 350–56.

14. Thomas N. Corns, "Milton's *Observations upon the Articles of Peace:* Ireland under English Eyes," in Loewenstein and Turner, *Politics, Poetics and Hermeneutics*, 124–25.

15. Peter Lake, "Anti-Popery: The Structure of a Prejudice," in *Conflict in Early Stuart England: Studies in Religion and Politics 1603–1642,* ed. Richard Cust and Ann Hughes (London and New York: Longman, 1989), 82.

16. Morley, *Remonstrance,* 6, 7, 12.

17. "The Solemn League and Covenant," in *The Constitutional Documents of the Puritan Revolution 1625–1660,* ed. Samuel Rawson Gardiner, 3d ed. (1906; reprint, Oxford: Clarendon Press, 1979), 268, 269.

18. John Buchan, *Oliver Cromwell* (1934; London: Hodder and Stoughton, 1935), 351–52, 353.

19. In the first 10 quarto pages of the first editions of the tracts, "I" and "me," taken together occur once in *Observations* and 13 times in *Eikonoklastes.*

20. John Peacock, "The Politics of Portraiture," in *Culture and Politics in Early Stuart England,* ed. Kevin Sharpe and Peter Lake (Basingstoke: Macmillan, 1994), 109.

21. Peacock, 226–27.

22.   My account follows the narrative in Masson, *Life,* II, 336–45.

23.   *Eikon Basilike* (n.p., 1649), 12–16; all references are to a copy in the library of the University of Wales, Bangor (shelfmark RS 942.062; Wing E268).

24.   For a fuller account, see Corns, *Uncloistered Virtue,* 80–91.

25.   Milton's account accords well, for example, with *A Declaration of the House of Commons* (London, 1642), usefully quoted at some length in *CPW,* III, 380, n. 16.

26.   For a larger account of the role of such stereotypes, see T. N. Corns, W. A. Speck, and J. A. Downie, "Archetypal Mystification: Polemic and Reality in English Political Literature, 1640–1750," *Eighteenth Century Life,* VII (1982), 1–27; the matter is more briefly considered in Corns, *Uncloistered Virtue,* 3–7.

Chapter Six

1.   Parker, *Life,* II, 961–62, nn. 35, 36, for an account of Salmasius and of the publishing history of his book. My narrative relies on Parker's.

2.   French, II, 286.

3.   Parker, *Life,* I, 360.

4.   Readers will find a substantial portion in modern translation by Kathryn A. McEuen in *CPW,* IV.ii, 986–1035.

5.   Robert Thomas Fallon, *Milton in Government* (University Park: Pennsylvania State University Press, 1993), 73–88, has an excellent account of Anglo-Dutch diplomatic relations as they touch on Milton's work for the republican government.

6.   Salmasius's phrase was "de parricidio apud Anglos in persona Regis," quoted *CPW,* IV.i, 310, n. 23, which usefully discusses the issues; see also *A Latin Dictionary,* ed. Charlton T. Lewis and Charles Short (1879; reprint, Oxford: Clarendon Press, 1927), s. v. "persona."

7.   *CPW,* IV.i, 542–43.

8.   French, III, 255.

9.   Ibid., 245; CPW, IV.i, 541.

10.   Godfrey Davies, *The Early Stuarts 1603–1660,* 2d ed. (Oxford: Oxford University Press, 1959), 224.

11.   Fallon, *Milton and Government,* 67.

12.   French, III, 357.

13.   Quoted from the journal of Bulstrode Whitelocke, the English ambassador in *CPW,* IV.i, 237.

14.   "Selections from Du Moulin, *Regii Sanguinis Clamor,*" trans. Paul W. Blackford, *CPW,* IV.ii, 1050.

15.   David Loewenstein, "Milton and the Poetics of Defense," in Loewenstein and Turner, *Politics, Poetics, and Hermeneutics,* 172.

16.   "The Printer in His Own Behalf," *The Public Faith of Alexander More,* translated by Paul W. Blackford, *CPW,* IV.ii, 1093.

Chapter Seven

1. For a lucid and graphic narrative, see Ronald Hutton, *The Restoration: A Political and Religious History of England and Wales 1658–1667* (Oxford: Clarendon Press, 1985; Oxford: Oxford University Press, 1987), 134; there is a ghastly contemporary illustration in Laura Lunger Knoppers, *Historicizing Milton: Spectacle, Power, and Poetry in Restoration England* (Athens, Ga., and London: University of Georgia Press, 1994), 54.

2. *The Journal of George Fox,* edited from the manuscript by Norman Penney (1911; reprint, New York: Octagon Books, 1973), I, 385; I have modernized spelling and punctuation in the interests of clarity.

3. For some consideration of the issue, see Thomas N. Corns, " 'No Man's Copy': The Critical Problem of Fox's *Journal,*" *Prose Studies* 17, no. 3 (1994): 99–111; reprinted in *The Emergence of Quaker Writing: Dissenting Literature in Seventeenth-Century England,* ed. Thomas N. Corns and David Loewenstein (London: Cass, 1995), 99–111.

4. Austin Woolrych, *Commonwealth to Protectorate* (Oxford: Clarendon Press, 1982), 236.

5. Woolrych, *Commonwealth to Protectorate,* 236–37.

6. *Poems,* 326–27.

7. Ibid., 328–29.

8. On controversies about tithes, see Worden, *Rump,* 201, 293; on tithes controversy in 1659, see *CPW,* VII, 77–83, and Hutton, *The Restoration,* 72–73.

9. Corns, *Development,* 6–19, 43–65.

10. *CPW,* VII, 77.

11. Ibid., 89.

12. He means the Waldensians, the proto-Protestant denomination whose massacre Milton had lamented in his "Sonnet XV. On the late Massacre in Piedmont" (*Poems,* 411–12). The group may have originated in Lyons as followers of Peter Waldo (*CPW,* VII, 302, n. 66).

13. See, for example, Steven Marx, "The Prophet Disarmed: Milton and the Quakers," *Studies in English Literature* 32 (1992): 111–28.

14. Hutton, *Restoration,* 47.

15. Ibid., 21–124.

16. Hill, *Milton,* 199.

17. Corns, *Uncloistered Virtue,* 271–93.

18. Sharpe, *Personal Rule,* 213–19.

19. Ibid., 218.

20. *CPW,* VII, 425, n. 91. See also *The English Court from the Wars of the Roses to the Civil War,* ed. David Starkey (London and New York: Longman, 1987), 1, 114, 135, 149–50, 178, 181, 186–88. Although the Groom of the Stool characteristically had a larger role in the royal administration, he retained a lavatorial responsibility.

21. Sharpe, *Personal Rule,* 127–28.

22. Hill, *God's Englishman,* 196; Cromwell made some change in his personal style late in life, which Hill attributes to political necessities, real or imagined.

23. Fox, *Journal,* I, 259–60.

24. Leo Miller, *John Milton and the Oldenburg Safeguard* (New York: Loewenthal Press, 1985), 41–42.

25. Corns, "An SPSS-Based Account."

26. For a vivid account, see *The Diary of Samuel Pepys,* ed. Robert Latham and William Matthews (London: Bell, 1970), I, 265.

Chapter Eight

1. *CPW,* VIII, 412; the preface by Keith W. F. Stavely contextualizes the tract very effectively.

2. *CPW,* VIII, 410.

3. Ronald Hutton, *Charles II: King of England, Scotland, and Ireland* (Oxford: Clarendon Press, 1989; Oxford: Oxford University Press, 1991), 275; my account owes much to his splendid narrative of events, especially his chapters 10 and 11.

4. Hutton, *Charles II,* 298.

5. See, for example, Sir Joseph Williamson's so-called spy-book, an alphabetical manuscript file on dissenter activists and their meeting places, Public Record Office, PRO SP 9/26.

6. Hutton, *Charles II,* 301.

7. George F. Sensabaugh, *That Grand Whig Milton* (Stanford: Stanford University Press; London: Oxford University Press, 1952; New York: Blum, 1967); Nicholas von Maltzahn, "The Whig Milton, 1667–1700," *in Milton and Republicanism,* 229–53.

8. Von Maltzahn, "The Whig Milton," 231.

9. *CPW,* VIII, 185; my account of the sources of the *Logic* rests heavily on Ong.

10. See, especially, Nicholas von Maltzahn, *Milton's History of Britain: Republican Historiography in the English Revolution* (Oxford: Clarendon Press, 1991), and Graham Parry's introduction to Milton's *The History of Britain* (Stamford: Paul Watkins, 1991).

11. Von Maltzahn, *Milton's* History, 26.

12. Graham Parry, *The Triumph of Time: English Antiquarians of the Seventeenth Century* (Oxford and New York: Oxford University Press, 1995).

13. Von Maltzahn, *Milton's* History, 53.

14. See Christopher Hill, *Puritanism and Revolution: Studies in Interpretation of the English Revolution of the 17th Century* (London: Secker and Warburg, 1958; London: Panther, 1969), chap. 3.

15. Von Maltzahn, *Milton's* History,13.

16. Von Maltzahn, *Milton's* History, chap. 1.

17. See the discussion of *De Doctrina Christiana* later in the chapter.

18. *CPW,* VIII, 463.

19. Ibid., 458.

20. Bodleian MS Rawl, A 185 fols. 271–74. James H. Hanford first noticed the personal connection between Skinner's family and Pepys in "Pepys and the Skinner Family," *Review of English Studies* 7 (1931): 251–70.

21. PRO 29/386/65.

22. See Elzevir to Skinner Sr., PRO SP 84/204/123–24 and 84/204/246–47.

23. *Dictionary of National Biography,* s.n. "Pitt, Moses."

24. Williamson to Meredith, PRO SP 104/66/120.

25. Meredith to Williamson, PRO SP 84/204/97–98, 84/294/102–3, 84/204/108–9, 84/204/140–41; Meredith obviously regarded the matter, initiated as it apparently was by the personal interest of Charles II, as meriting some words of report in almost every dispatch through February 1677, among issues of grave diplomatic and military significance.

26. For early and influential attempts to negotiate the issues of the relationship between the treatise and Milton's undisputed oeuvre, see Maurice Kelley, *This Great Argument: A Study of Milton's "De Doctrina Christiana" as a Gloss upon "Paradise Lost"* (Princeton: Princeton University Press, 1941); Barbara Lewalski, *Milton's Brief Epic: The Genre, Meaning, and Art of "Paradise Regained"* (Providence, R.I.: Brown University Press; London: Methuen, 1966); Mary Ann Radzinowicz, *Toward "Samson Agonistes": The Growth of Milton's Mind* (Princeton: Princeton University Press, 1978); and W. B. Hunter, C. A. Patrides, and J. H. Adamson, *Bright Essence: Studies in Milton's Theology* (Salt Lake City: University of Utah Press, 1971). W. B. Hunter's more recent view is developed in a series of papers, "The Provenance of *Christian Doctrine,*" *Studies in English Literature* (hereafter *SEL*) 32 (1992): 129–42 (first delivered at the Fourth International Milton Symposium, Vancouver, 1991); "The Provenance of *Christian Doctrine*: Addenda from the Bishop of Salisbury," *SEL* 33 (1993): 191–207; and "Animadversions upon the Remonstrants' Defences against Burgess and Hunter," *SEL,* forthcoming.

27. See Barbara Lewalski, John T. Shawcross, and William B. Hunter, "Forum: Milton's *Christian Doctrine,*" *SEL* 32 (1992): 143–66; Maurice Kelley, Christopher Hill, and William B. Hunter, "Forum II: Milton's *Christian Doctrine,*" SEL 34 (1994): 153–93.

28. Michael Bauman, *A Scripture Index to John Milton's* De doctrina christiana (Binghampton: MRTS, 1989), 175.

29. Since 1994 I have been working with a multidisciplinary group on the issue of the provenance of *De Doctrina Christiana;* the account I have given of the nature of the problem rests largely on Gordon Campbell, Thomas N. Corns, and John K. Hale, "The Provenance of *De Doctrina Christiana:* An Interim Report," British Milton Seminar, March 1994, and Gordon Campbell,

Thomas N. Corns, John K. Hale, David Holmes, and Fiona Tweedie, "The Provenance of *De Doctrina Christiana:* A Second Interim Report," Fifth International Milton Symposium, Bangor, 1995; "the third hypothesis" is demonstrated in Gordon Campbell, Thomas N. Corns, John K. Hale, David Holmes, and Fiona Tweedie, "The Provenance of *De Doctrina Christiana:* A Final Report," British Milton Seminar, October 1996, and to be published in *Milton Quarterly*. I am indebted to my colleagues in the research group.

Selected Bibliography

PRIMARY WORKS

Milton, John. *The Works of John Milton.* Edited by Frank Allen Patterson et al. 18 vols. New York: Columbia University Press, 1931–1938. This edition is not annotated significantly except for textual aspects, but it does have a superb two-volume index. It prints the Latin texts in their original language, with a parallel English translation.

Milton, John. *Complete Prose Works of John Milton.* Edited by Don M. Wolfe et al. 8 vols. New Haven: Yale University Press, 1953–1982. This edition is heavily annotated, and each volume has a long introduction, largely concerned with historical contextualization. Latin works appear only in English translation.

Milton, John. *Selected Prose.* Edited by C. A. Patrides. Rev. ed. Columbia: University of Missouri Press, 1985. This edition, the best among selected and less scholarly editions, contains a 30-page bibliography.

Milton, John. *Political Writings.* Cambridge Texts in the History of Political Thought, ed. Martin Dzelzainis. Cambridge: Cambridge University Press, 1991. A generous selection, with a singularly valuable introduction.

SECONDARY WORKS

Reference Works

Hunter, William B., ed. *A Milton Encyclopedia.* 9 vols. Lewisburg, Pa.: Bucknell University Press, 1978–1983. A useful guide to many aspects of Milton's life and work.

Sterne, Laurence, and Harold Kollmeier. *Concordance to the English Prose of John Milton.* Binghamton: MRTS, 1985. An excellent resource for finding material in the prose oeuvre.

Bibliographies

Huckaby, Calvin. *John Milton: An Annotated Bibliography, 1929–1968.* Rev. ed. Pittsburgh: Duquesne University Press, 1969.

Klemp, Paul J. *The Essential Milton: An Annotated Critical Bibliography of Major Modern Studies.* Boston: G. K. Hall, 1989.

Patrides, C. A. *An Annotated Critical Bibliography of John Milton.* Brighton: Harvester, 1987.

Shawcross, John T. *Milton: A Bibliography for the Years 1624–1700*. Binghamton: MRTS, 1984. Provides a guide to earlier material relating to Milton's writing.

Biographies, Life Records, and Chronology

Campbell, Gordon. *A Milton Chronology*. London and Basingstoke: Macmillan; Lanham: Barnes and Noble, 1997. This text incorporates new material that has appeared since the publication of French's *Life Records*, which it emends and supplements in many ways.

French, J. Milton. *The Life Records of John Milton*. 5 vols. New Brunswick, N.J.: Rutgers University Press, 1949–1958. Reprint,. New York: Gordian Press, 1966. This text records chronologically a mass of documentation relating to Milton's life and to the publication and reception of his works.

Parker, William Riley. *Milton: A Biography and a Biographical Commentary*. Revised by Gordon Campbell. 2d ed. 2 vols. Oxford: Clarendon Press, 1996. Campbell incorporates recent research into Parker's richly documented account. This text is currently the best biography.

Shawcross, John T. *John Milton: The Self and the World*. Lexington: University of Kentucky Press, 1993. A challenging and controversial interpretation, resting heavily on twentieth-century psychoanalytical assumptions.

Wilson, A. N. *The Life of John Milton*. Oxford: Oxford University Press, 1983. Slighter, much less scholarly, and somewhat speculative, but a highly readable account.

Milton and His Age

Corns, Thomas N. *Uncloistered Virtue: English Political Literature 1640–1660*. Oxford: Clarendon Press, 1992. Contains four long chapters on Milton's political prose.

Hill, Christopher. *Milton and the English Revolution*. London: Faber and Faber, 1977. Particularly strong on the ideological connections that Hill notices between Milton and other radical thinkers.

———. *The Experience of Defeat: Milton and Some Contemporaries*. London: Faber and Faber, 1984. Focuses poignantly on his later years.

Milner, Andrew. *John Milton and the English Revolution*. London and Basingstoke: Macmillan, 1981. Particularly strong on locating Milton's thought within Revolutionary Independency.

Smith, Nigel. *Literature and Revolution in England 1640–1660*. New Haven and London: Yale University Press, 1994. Milton figures prominently in a richly detailed account of the impact of politics on literary history.

Other Books on the Historical Context

Hughes, Ann. *The Causes of the English Civil War*. Basingstoke and London: Macmillan, 1991. A judicious evaluation of alternative hypotheses and the best short book on the origins of the Civil War.

Sharpe, Kevin. *The Personal Rule of Charles I.* New Haven and London: Yale University Press, 1992. A monumental study of the late 1620s and the 1630s.

Underdown, David E. *Pride's Purge: Politics in the Puritan Revolution.* Oxford: Clarendon Press, 1971. The best account of the purging of the Long Parliament, the judicial process against the King, and the establishment of the republic.

Woolrych, Austin. *Commonwealth to Protectorate.* Oxford: Clarendon Press, 1982. An informative text on the collapse of the early republican form of government.

The work of Christopher Hill has shaped the way generations of critics have regarded the crises of the mid–seventeenth century. His books have been frequently reprinted. See especially

Hill, Christopher. *Puritanism and Revolution.* London: Secker and Warburg, 1958.

———. *The Century of Revolution 1603–1714.* London: Thomas Nelson, 1961.

———. *God's Englishman: Oliver Cromwell and the English Revolution.* London: Weidenfeld and Nicholson, 1970.

———. *The World Turned Upside Down: Radical Ideas during the English Revolution.* London: Maurice Temple Smith, 1972.

On the conflicts between episcopalians and their critics, see

Davies, Julian. *The Caroline Captivity of the Church: Charles I and the Remolding of Anglicanism 1625–1641.* Oxford: Clarendon Press, 1992.

Tyacke, Nicholas. *Anti-Calvinists: The Rise of English Arminianism, c. 1590–1640.* Oxford: Clarendon Press, 1987.

On the end of the republic and on the Puritans' fate in the early years of the Restoration, see

Hutton, Ronald. *The Restoration: A Political and Religious History of England and Wales, 1658–1667.* Oxford: Clarendon Press, 1985, reprint 1987.

———. *Charles II: King of England, Scotland, and Ireland.* Oxford: Oxford University Press, 1989, reprint 1991.

Critical Responses

GENERAL

Achinstein, Sharon. *Milton and the Revolutionary Reader.* Princeton: Princeton University Press, 1994. Particularly acute discussions of *Areopagitica* and *Eikonoklastes.*

Corns, Thomas N. *The Development of Milton's Prose Style.* Oxford: Clarendon Press, 1982. The only methodologically sound book-length account of his prose style.

Egan, James. *The Inward Teacher: Milton's Rhetoric of Christian Liberty.* University Park, Pa.: Seventeenth-Century News, 1980. An account of the larger rhetorical structures.

Loewenstein, David. *Milton and the Drama of History: Historical Vision, Iconoclasm, and the Literary Imagination.* Cambridge: Cambridge University Press, 1990. Fine readings, especially of *Of Reformation, Areopagitica,* the *Defences,* and *Eikonoklastes.*

Nyquist, Mary, and Margaret W. Ferguson, eds. *Re-membering Milton: Essays on the Texts and Traditions.* New York and London: Methuen, 1987. A multiply authored collection that has important essays, especially on *Areopagitica* and the divorce tracts.

Skerpan, Elizabeth. *The Rhetoric of Politics in the English Revolution 1642–1660.* Columbia and London: University of Missouri Press, 1992. Particularly valuable in its contextualization of Milton's rhetoric in contemporary practice.

Stavely, Keith W. *The Politics of Milton's Prose Style.* New Haven: Yale University Press, 1975. Considers points of contrast between Milton's expository techniques and those of other radical writers.

Two very significant and influential collections of essays by several hands are

Lieb, Michael, and John T. Shawcross, eds. *Achievements of the Left Hand: Essays on the Prose of John Milton.* Amherst: University of Massachusetts Press, 1974.

Loewenstein, David, and James Grantham Turner, eds. *Politics, Poetics, and Hermeneutics in Milton's Prose.* Cambridge: Cambridge University Press, 1990.

THE ANTIPRELATICAL PAMPHLETS

Anselment, Raymond A. *"Betwixt Jest and Earnest": Marprelate, Milton, Marvell, Swift and the Decorum of Religious Ridicule.* Toronto, Buffalo, and London: University of Toronto Press, 1979.

Egan, James. "Milton and the Marprelate Tradition." *Milton Studies* 8 (1975): 103–21.

Kranidas, Thomas. "Milton and the Rhetoric of Zeal." *Texas Studies in Language and Literature* 6 (1965): 423–32.

———. " 'Decorum' and the Style of Milton's Antiprelatical Tracts." *Studies in Philology* 62 (1965): 176–87; reprinted in Stanley Fish, ed. *Seventeenth Century Prose: Modern Essays in Criticism,* 475–88. New York: Oxford University Press, 1971.

———. "Milton's *Of Reformation*: The Politics of Vision." *English Literary History* 49 (1982): 497–513.

———. "Words, Words, Words, and the Word: Milton's *Of Prelaticall Episcopacy.*" *Milton Studies* 16 (1982): 153–66.

———. "Style and Rectitude in Seventeenth-Century Prose: Hall, Smectymnuus, and Milton." *Huntington Library Quarterly* 46 (1983): 237–69.

Milton's early prose is the subject of analysis in chapters of two of the most profoundly influential studies of the early modern period:

Fish, Stanley E. *Self-Consuming Artifacts: The Experience of Seventeenth-Century Literature.* Berkeley, Los Angeles, and London: University of California Press, 1972.
Webber, Joan. *The Eloquent "I": Style and Self in Seventeenth-Century Prose.* Madison and London: University of Wisconsin Press, 1968.

THE DIVORCE TRACTS AND *AREOPAGITICA*

Illo, John. "*Areopagiticas* Mythic and Real." *Prose Studies* 11 (1988): 3–23. Questions the status of the tract as liberal icon.
Kranidas, Thomas. "Polarity and Structure in Milton's *Areopagitica.*" *English Literary Renaissance* 14 (1984): 234–54. A good reading of its larger rhetorical configuration.
Turner, James Grantham. *One Flesh: Paradisal Marriage and Sexual Relations in the Age of Milton.* Oxford: Clarendon Press, 1987. A brilliant account of Miltonic representations of sexuality in the context of contemporary opinion.
Wilding, Michael. "Milton's *Areopagitica*: Liberty for the Sects." *Prose Studies* 9, no. 2 (1986): 7–38. Reprinted in Thomas N. Corns, ed. *The Literature of Controversy: Polemical Strategy from Milton to Junius,* 7–38. London: Cass, 1987. Very alert to the ideological aspects of Milton's imagery.

THE TRACTS OF 1649, STATE PAPERS, AND THE LATIN *DEFENSES*

Armitage, David, Armand Himy, and Quentin Skinner, eds. *Milton and Republicanism.* Cambridge: Cambridge University Press, 1995. Contains several important discussions of the Latin and English prose.
Fallon, Robert T. *Milton in Government.* University Park: Pennsylvania State University Press, 1993. Complements and extends Miller's work.
Miller, Leo. *John Milton and the Oldenburg Safeguard: New Light on Milton and his Friends in the Commonwealth from the Diaries and Letters of Hermann Mylius, Agonist in the Early History of Modern Diplomacy.* New York: Loewenthal Press, 1985. An insider view of Milton's role in the civil service of republican England.
Zwicker, Steven N. *Lines of Authority: Politics and English Literary Culture, 1649–1689.* Ithaca, N.Y., and London: Cornell University Press, 1993. Has a good chapter on *Eikonoklastes* and *Eikon Basilike.*

THE TRACTS OF 1659–1660

Holstun, James. *A Rational Millennium: Puritan Utopias of Seventeenth-Century England and America.* New York and Oxford: Clarendon Press, 1987. Particularly interesting on *The Readie and Easie Way*.
Lewalski, Barbara Kiefer. "Milton: Political Beliefs and Polemical Method, 1659–60." *PMLA: Proceedings of the Modern Language Association of Amer-*

ica 74 (1959): 191–202. A terse, assured, and convincing account of the whole cluster of pamphlets.

On the revisions to *The Readie and Easie Way,* see

Ayers, Robert W. "The Editions of *Readie & Easie Way.*" *Review of English Studies* 25 (1974): 280–91.
Stewart, Stanley. "Milton Revises *The Readie and Easie Way.*" *Milton Studies* 20 (1984): 205–24.

MISCELLANEOUS AND POSTHUMOUS PUBLICATIONS

Bauman, Michael. *A Scripture Index to John Milton's* De doctrina christiana. Binghamton: MRTS, 1989. A singularly useful tool for locating biblical texts within the treatise.
Hunter, W. B., C. A. Patrides, and J. H. Adamson. *Bright Essence: Studies in Milton's Theology.* Salt Lake City: University of Utah Press, 1971. A concerted attempt to reconcile *Christian Doctrine* with Milton's poetry.
Kelley, Maurice. *This Great Argument: A Study of Milton's "De Doctrina Christiana" as a Gloss upon "Paradise Lost."* Princeton: Princeton University Press, 1941. The classic argument for the place of the treatise in Milton's work.
Parry, Graham. Introduction to *The History of Britain, by* John Milton. Stamford: Paul Watkins, 1991. The facsimile is of minor critical interest, but Parry's introduction is terse, lucid, and shows a fine understanding of Milton's place in English historiography.
Sanchez, Reuben Marquez, Jr. " 'The Worst of Superstitions': Milton's *Of True Religion* and the Issue of Religious Tolerance." *Prose Studies* 9 (1986): 21–38. A good starting point; many aspects of this tract merit further consideration.
von Maltzahn, Nicholas. *Milton's* History of Britain: *Republican Historiography in the English Revolution.* Oxford: Clarendon Press, 1991. Assured, authoritative; easily the best work on the subject.

On the controversy about the provenance of *Christian Doctrine,* see

Campbell, Gordon, Thomas N. Corns, John K. Hale, David Holmes, and Fiona Tweedie. "The Provenance of *De Doctrina Christiana*: A Final Report." *Milton Quarterly,* forthcoming.
Hunter, W. B. "The Provenance of *Christian Doctrine.*" *Studies in English Literature* 32 (1992): 129–42.
———. "The Provenance of *Christian Doctrine*: Addenda from the Bishop of Salisbury." *Studies in English Literature* 33 (1993): 191–207.
———. "Animadversions upon the Remonstrants' Defenses against Burgess and Hunter." *Studies in English Literature* 34 (1994): 195–203.

Kelley, Maurice, Christopher Hill, and William B. Hunter. "Forum II: Milton's *Christian Doctrine.*" *Studies in English Literature* 34 (1994): 153–93.

Lewalski, Barbara, John T. Shawcross, and William B. Hunter. "Forum: Milton's *Christian Doctrine.*" *Studies in English Literature* 32 (1992): 143–66.

Index

The Author

Thomas N. Corns is professor of English and head of the School of English and Linguistics at the University of Wales, Bangor. He was educated at Brasenose and University Colleges, Oxford, and the Maximilianeum Foundation, Munich. His principal publications include *The Development of Milton's Prose Style* (Oxford: Clarendon Press, 1982), *Milton's Language* (Oxford: Blackwell, 1990), *Uncloistered Virtue: English Political Literature, 1640–1660* (Oxford: Clarendon Press, 1992), and *Regaining "Paradise Lost"* (London and New York: Longman, 1994). He edited *The Cambridge Companion to English Poetry, Donne to Marvell* (Cambridge: Cambridge University Press, 1993). He is the British editor of *Prose Studies*.

The Editor

Arthur F. Kinney is the Thomas W. Copeland Professor of Literary History at the University of Massachusetts, Amherst, and the director of the Center for Renaissance Studies there; he is also an adjunct professor of English at New York University. He has written several books in the field: *Humanist Poetics, Continental Humanist Poetics, John Skelton: Priest as Poet,* and the forthcoming *Lies Like the Truth: 'Macbeth' and the Cultural Moment* are among them. He is the founding editor of the journal *English Literary Renaissance* and editor of the book series, "Massachusetts Studies in Early Modern Culture."